"While on active duty at the Bamberg US Army Base in Germany, I saw hundreds of soldiers returning from Iraq and Afghanistan with combat and operational stress reaction (COSR). In my professional opinion, the mind-body bridging technique featured in *Mind-Body Workbook for PTSD* is the single most effective method for the treatment PTSD and COSR."

> —Major Philip Davis, Ph.D., US Army Reserve

"Without the mind-body bridging tools in *Mind-Body Workbook for PTSD*, I would be dead. Not only has it saved my life, but made it better than it was before I was deployed."

> —Sergeant First Class Kip Day, Utah National Guard and combat veteran
> of Operation Iraqi Freedom

"Drawing upon recent advances in the field of trauma recovery, the authors have created a unique holistic approach to helping trauma survivors. Their step-by-step method of helping readers better understand and cope with the all-important mind-body connection and its relationship to the low self-esteem, anxiety, anger, sleeping difficulties, and other common emotional, physical, social, and mental aftereffects of trauma, is truly brilliant."

> —Aphrodite Matsakis, Ph.D., author of *I Can't Get Over It, Trust After Trauma,*
> and eight other books on trauma

"This scientifically sound and comprehensive *Mind-Body Workbook for PTSD* has broken new ground by offering highly effective strategies for mental health treatment. In my twenty years of clinical experience working with complex PTSD and other mental disorders, I have found mind-body bridging, the method taught in this self-help book, to be the most tolerated and effective treatment approach among other evidence-based models, including cognitive processing therapy, cognitive behavior therapy, dialectical behavior therapy, prolonged exposure, and eye movement desensitization and reprocessing. Results have been impressive compared to the evidence-based treatments used in my practice. This workbook is compelling and instructive in its ability to help clients develop sufficient resources for sustainable self-healing and empowerment. I have been using mind-body bridging for the past three years in individual and group treatments. I have treated over 100 clients using mind-body bridging and have had no clients terminate treatment."

> —Lois Waldron, LCSW, Springfield, MA

D1088284

MIND-BODY WORKBOOK
for PTSD

PTSD

A 10-*Week Program for*
Healing After Trauma

STANLEY H. BLOCK, MD,
& CAROLYN BRYANT BLOCK

NEW HARBINGER PUBLICATIONS, INC.

Publisher's Note

Distributed in Canada by Raincoast Books

Copyright © 2010 by Stanley H. Block & Carolyn Bryant Block
New Harbinger Publications, Inc.
5674 Shattuck Avenue
Oakland, CA 94609
www.newharbinger.com

All Rights Reserved
Printed in the United States of America

Acquired by Jess O'Brien; Cover design by Amy Shoup; Edited by Nelda Street

FSC
Mixed Sources
Product group from well-managed
forests and other controlled sources

Cert no. SW-COC-002283
www.fsc.org
© 1996 Forest Stewardship Council

Library of Congress Cataloging-in-Publication Data

Block, Stanley H.
  Mind-body workbook for PTSD : a 10-week program for healing after trauma / Stanley H. Block and Carolyn Bryant Block.
      p. cm.
  Includes bibliographical references.
  ISBN 978-1-57224-923-3 (pbk.) -- ISBN 978-1-57224-924-0 (pdf ebook)
  1. Post-traumatic stress disorder--Treatment--Problems, exercises, etc. 2. Psychic trauma--Treatment--Problems, exercises, etc. 3. Mind and body--Problems, exercises, etc. I. Block, Carolyn Bryant. II. Title.
  RC552.P67B63 2010
  616.85'21--dc22

                    2010037595

13 12 11
10 9 8 7 6 5 4 3 2

Contents

ACKNOWLEDGMENTS

Our teaching about trauma is primarily influenced by the heroic way individuals suffering from trauma have shared with us the ways they used mind-body bridging to free themselves from the past. Although we have not specifically referenced other trauma workers, we appreciate their pioneering work and have used many of their concepts, such as secondary wounding and trauma triggers. The clinicians using, developing, and refining mind-body bridging have our gratitude. Deserving of specific mention is Rich Landward, a gifted trauma expert who developed most of the advanced PTSD maps and whose feedback guided this workbook's development. Don Glover, Harold Price, Kevin Webb, Theresa McCormick, and Joe Boberg have all contributed significantly to this workbook. We greatly appreciate the research efforts of Yoshi Nakamura and Derrik Tollefson to establish a firm evidence basis for mind-body bridging. Carol Ann Kent expanded our ten-week generic plan into a workbook format. This work would not have been possible without the editorial supervision and skill of Andrea Peters. And finally, we found the direction from the editors of New Harbinger Publications to be most helpful.

INTRODUCTION

You can have a traumatic experience that's so horrible no one else in the world understands what you've been through. Rather than being healed and leaving a scar that blends into the past, your traumatic experience erupts again and again, disturbing every part of your life. Many times, this flare-up of uncontrolled thoughts, flashbacks, avoidance of certain situations, numb feelings, and need to be on high alert (hypervigilance) happens daily. Such flare-ups even happen at night, causing trouble sleeping, bad dreams, and even nightmares. These troubling symptoms leave you feeling irritable, angry, and alone. The past simply won't become the past, and life feels like hell! If this describes you, this workbook is for you.

TRAUMA, STRESS, AND POST-TRAUMATIC STRESS DISORDER

Trauma is a sudden, intense physical or emotional (or both) event that harms the person experiencing it. A trauma can be a single event or repeated events. We all have had traumatic experiences. They include: child abuse, childhood bullying, illness, accidents, domestic violence, rape, losses, natural disasters, and wartime situations. Our ability to heal from these experiences varies.

Stress is the body's signal that the traumatic event has drained our physical and emotional resources. Often stress from such past events goes away on its own. But in many cases, the symptoms of stress never go away, or they come back later. Sometimes the stress symptoms (such as intense fear or horror, helplessness, the need to avoid things, trouble sleeping, and irritability) disrupt our lives so much that they qualify for a clinical diagnosis.

After carefully studying the symptoms of trauma sufferers, psychiatrists have agreed on a category of diagnosis called *post-traumatic stress disorder* (*PTSD*). PTSD symptoms are present for at least one month after a stressful traumatic event that causes you significant problems with functioning in relationships, at work, or in other important areas of life.

Here's a brief description of these symptoms, as summarized from the *Diagnostic and Statistical Manual of Mental Disorders (DSM-IV-TR)* (APA 2000):

◆ Reexperiencing the trauma over and over such that it interferes with your daily life

◆ Avoiding thoughts, feelings, people, places, activities, or other reminders of the trauma, as well as losing interest in doing things you once enjoyed, feeling disconnected from others and unable to have loving feelings, and not expecting to live life in a normal way

◆ Having trouble sleeping, irritability, angry outbursts, and trouble concentrating, as well as being on guard and easily startled

CAN YOUR MIND-BODY HEAL ITSELF?

With hundreds of books on the subject and even more websites, PTSD is a well-studied condition. There's plenty of information about what PTSD is and what to do for it—but you don't need more information. So why write another book? This practical workbook is based on the fact that your *mind-body*—mind and body as a unified whole—knows how to heal itself after trauma. Sound radical? It is!

I'll bet you're thinking, *If I have this great healing power, why do I still have all these symptoms?* That's the most important question you could possibly ask. The latest in brain research (Boly et al. 2008a), along with over a decade of clinical experience from physicians, psychologists, social workers, and researchers (Tollefson et al. 2009), has given us the answer. When overactive, a system in our bodies known as the *Identity System* (*I-System*) disrupts our natural self-healing processes. This workbook gives you easy daily exercises that will help you recognize and defuse this interference, letting your self-healing process resume.

THE IDENTITY SYSTEM (I-SYSTEM)

Everyone has an I-System that's either active or resting (Block and Block 2007). The I-System is active when you have PTSD symptoms. You know the I-System is on when your mind is cluttered with spinning thoughts, your body is tense, your awareness shrinks, and you have trouble thinking or doing things. It's called the I-System because we falsely *identify with* the contents of the spinning thoughts and the physical distress they cause. It's crucial to recognize the I-System, because when it's active, it disrupts your body's natural regulation and healing. When you reexperience your trauma, when you're driven to avoid certain everyday situations, and when you're emotionally numb and on high alert, it's because your I-System is on. You live your everyday life and see the world through the pain of your PTSD. You will learn more about the I-System, in both its active and resting states, as you read on.

WHAT IS MIND-BODY BRIDGING?

Mind-body bridging uses both the mind and the body to build a bridge from a condition (state) of impaired healing to one in which they heal themselves. This workbook offers mind-body tools (techniques and practices) to quiet your I-System. As you will see for yourself, these tools are very easy to apply in your daily life, and they work quickly. In working with patients, we've found that when you are given tools aimed directly at quieting down the I-System, PTSD symptoms begin to naturally heal on their own (Nakamura et al. forthcoming). Mind-body bridging lets your self-healing resume.

BRAIN BASIS FOR MIND-BODY BRIDGING

Brain research (Weissman et al. 2006) has found two networks of functioning with different features: an executive network and a default-mode network. The *executive network* coordinates moment by moment how we see the world, think, make decisions, and act. It's responsible for the direction and management of our life. The *default-mode network* is at work when we're having exaggerated thoughts about ourselves and our experiences. We have a harder time responding to situations as they come up. Researchers have found that when the default-mode network is active, the executive network is inactive (Boly et al. 2008b). So only one network can be in the driver's seat at a time.

Using a technology called fMRI, scientists and doctors can now take pictures of how the brain changes while it's busy. Shaun Ho (Block, Ho, and Nakamura 2009) suggests that the I-System corresponds to the default-mode network, and mind-body bridging corresponds to the executive network. Brain research (Boly et al. 2008b) shows that when the default-mode network is not overactive, your executive network takes charge, regulating your mind so you function at your best. The I-System is responsible for keeping your PTSD symptoms going. In working with our patients, we find that mind-body bridging quiets the I-System, letting us heal ourselves from trauma.

Imagine a big switch in your brain that turns the I-System (default-mode network) on and off. When the I-System is on, it switches off your executive functioning. When the switch is off it rests, letting you heal and live life at its best.

MIND-BODY LANGUAGE

We will introduce you to a mind-body language that describes your personal experiences using simple terms, descriptive labels for states of your mind and body. They are not meant to carry deep psychological meaning, but they *can* give you the power to quickly start reducing your PTSD symptoms and take off on your self-healing journey.

For example, sometimes life is just hell. Your head is full of self-hating thoughts, your body screams out in misery, and nothing you do brings any relief. You can barely carry out your daily activities. This state of mind and body is the *damaged self*. The damaged self is not just a negative self-image; it also impairs every cell in your body. It is caused by the overactivity of your I-System and doesn't refer to decreased mental or physical functioning associated with injury, illness, trauma, a difficult childhood, or even your DNA.

When you use the tools in this workbook to calm your I-System, you will automatically to a state of natural harmony and balance in your life. This is your *true self.* In this mind-body state, you heal yourself. See the appendix for short definitions of these terms.

THIS BOOK HELPS EVERYONE

The tools in this workbook have proved to be successful even in extreme cases of stress, trauma, and PTSD. They work for men and women, people in the military and those who aren't. And they work even if you have another problem (such as a brain injury, pain, a sleep disorder, alcohol or substance abuse, or other mental disorders) along with PTSD. The most important feature of this workbook is that it's made for you, the individual reader, and relies 100 percent on your doing the exercises. You will learn to heal yourself.

HOW TO USE THIS BOOK

This workbook is a self-study course with ten chapters. With seven daily exercises, each chapter is designed for you to complete over one week. It's important to do the exercises in order. If you miss a day, review the chapter, look back at what you've done during the week, and pick up where you left off. It's important to keep up to date by using all the tools you've learned, because they are the groundwork for the next day's assignment. It can sometimes help to spend more than a week on a chapter. The key to healing successfully is to use your mind-body bridging tools in your daily routine. There's no gain in taking a vacation from living your life at its best.

At the end of each chapter is an MBB (Mind-Body Bridging) Weekly Evaluation Scale that helps you measure your progress in using your practices in your daily life. Healing takes place over time. You will learn about and heal yourself at your own pace. If you get a low score in a certain area on the scale, go over the exercise related to that item. Doing well on these weekly scales means you are changing your life. Also, there are three MBB Quality of Life Scales in this book, which help you see your progress in healing.

CHAPTER 1

SELF-DISCOVERY AND
SELF-HEALING OF PTSD

In this first chapter, let's start with a quick two-part exercise. If you follow the instructions, you'll see how well and how quickly the tools work. In just a few pages, you'll see that the expert in healing your trauma is standing in your shoes—right here, right now. Only after doing this exercise and showing yourself that you have the ability to heal yourself should you start your ten-week journey of daily exercises. Your first week will show you that you can use everyday activities to improve your life.

DAY ONE   DATE: _____

1. Take a problem that's bothering you right now, and write it in the following oval. It may help to look at the sample map on the next page. Next, take a couple of minutes to write whatever thoughts come to mind about your problem, scattering them around the oval. Be as specific as possible, working quickly and without editing your thoughts.

PROBLEM MAP

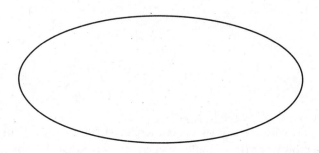

a. Is your mind clear, or is it cluttered with thoughts?

_____

b. Is your body relaxed or tense? List where and how your body is tense:

_____

_____

c. With your mind and body in this condition, how do you act?

_____

_____

We bet you believe your troubling problem is what's creating all the commotion in your life, which you can see on your map. It's not! You have just experienced your I-System at work. Your I-System grabs your thoughts, creates mind clutter and body tension, and influences your actions. The map in step 2 will teach you how to control your I-System.

SAMPLE PROBLEM MAP

This isn't the way the world should be.

No one ever says thank you.

It's depressing.

They make me mad.

People are rude.

People cut in line.

People don't help each other anymore.

Jack shows me no respect.

a. Is your mind clear or cluttered with thoughts?

My mind is so cluttered with thoughts about others that I forget about me.

b. Is your body tense or relaxed? List where and how your body is tense:

Tight shoulders, "band" around my head, stomachache, really tense all over

c. With your mind and body in this condition, how do you act?

Irritable, angry; have to stop myself from punching someone

Chapter 1—Day One cont.

2. The next part of this exercise can change your life forever, because it shows you how to get your I-System to rest. For this important activity, it would help to be in a room without such distractions as the radio, TV, or people talking. Write the same problem (the one you wrote down in the first map) in the next oval. Before you continue, seat yourself comfortably, listen to any background sounds, experience your body's pressure on your seat, feel your feet on the floor, and feel the pen in your hand. If you have thoughts, gently return to listening to background sounds and tuning in to your senses. Once you feel settled, start writing whatever comes to mind about the problem. Watch the ink go onto the paper, keep feeling the pen in your hand, and listen to any background sounds. Write for three to four minutes.

PROBLEM MAP WITH BRIDGING

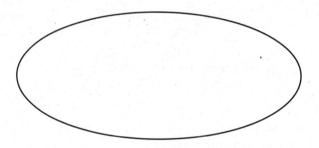

a. Is your mind clear or cluttered with thoughts?

_____

b. Is your body relaxed or tense?

_____

_____

c. How is this map different from the first one you made?

_____

_____

d. Do you feel clearer about your problem now? Yes _____ No _____

e. If you could live your life with your mind-body in this state, do you think it would enhance your self-healing powers? Yes _____ No _____

Chapter 1—Day One cont.

This first exercise was an activity called *mind-body mapping*. Mind-body maps are short writing exercises that take no longer than a few minutes and, like doodling, serve as little snapshots of your thoughts and level of body tension. The first map helped you to see your I-System's activity, while the second map let you experience the benefits of when your I-System is quiet.

Take a look at the differences between your two completed maps. Just as a cut on your finger will naturally heal, your PTSD will naturally heal if the mental and physical commotion of your I-System calms down. Whether it was a knife, saw, glass, or ax that wounded you, your body's responsibility is to heal, no matter what the cause. In the second map, you saw firsthand what it's like to calm your I-System. You saw that when you literally come to your senses by focusing on your body sensations and the sounds around you, the I-System calms, and you can better deal with your problem. Throughout the workbook you will learn mind-body bridging tools to quiet your I-System. Mind-body bridging uses the mind and body to move you from your damaged self to your healing, naturally functioning true self. Natural functioning is how you think, feel, see the world, and act when your I-System is quiet.

This week you will use in your daily life what you learned from the two maps you made today. The most important part of this workbook is your doing the exercises. With each exercise come more tools for your toolbox. It's important to do each exercise as it comes in the workbook; this builds a solid foundation for successfully reducing your trauma or PTSD symptoms. Your results depend solely on your ability to use in everyday life what you learn. Your ability to heal yourself grows on its own. You don't need to force yourself to heal, any more than you need to force a cut finger to heal. Once you learn to quiet your I-System, healing takes place naturally.

Many people suffering from PTSD come back after the first session and say, "I still have my symptoms, but my house is getting bigger." This analogy of having a bigger living space is exactly how mind-body bridging works. When you quiet your I-System as you did in the second map, you automatically resume a more settled state and your ability to handle problems has grown (as shown in figure 1.1). Note that the size of the problem or symptoms hasn't changed. People suffering from PTSD come to believe that the small vessel filled with symptoms is all that they are. They have lived their lives limited by mental and physical pain. Simply by quieting your I-System, you become an expanded vessel. Your living space, healing space, and problem-solving space expand with mind-body bridging so your natural healing state can resume.

It's important to do each exercise as it comes in the workbook; this builds a solid foundation for successfully reducing your trauma or PTSD symptoms.

Fill out your first MBB Quality of Life Scale at the end of today's exercises. We have placed this scale throughout your workbook so you can objectively note your progress and systematically keep track of your life-changing experience.

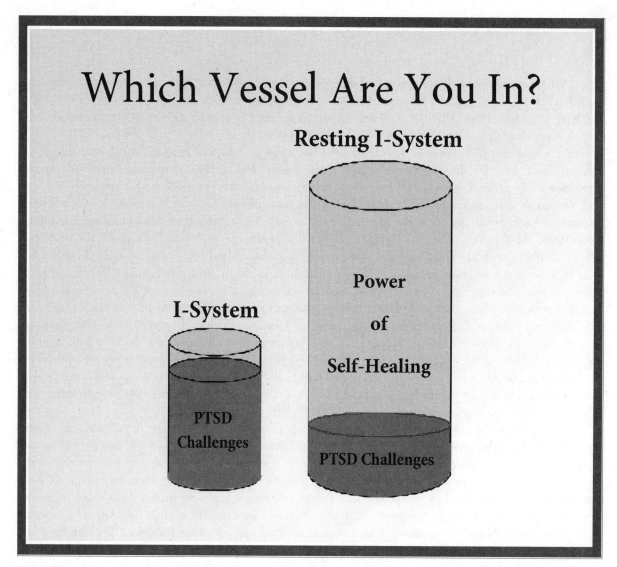

Figure 1.1

As we mentioned, when living with PTSD challenges, we see ourselves as the small vessel. We have falsely come to believe that the small vessel filled with symptoms (the dark shaded area) is *all* we are, with limited space (in the lightly shaded area) for anything else. It's the overactive I-System that keeps us there.

We automatically expand into a bigger vessel when the I-System is resting. The lightly shaded area represents our living space, our problem-solving space, and our healing space. The size of your challenges hasn't changed, but the size of the vessel has. The lightly shaded area in the larger vessel expands as you quiet your I-System with mind-body bridging tools, putting you in a state where healing can happen.

MBB Quality of Life Scale

Date: _____

Fill out your first MBB Quality of Life Scale. We have placed this scale throughout your workbook so you can objectively note your progress and systematically keep track of your life-changing experience.

Over the past seven days, how did you do in these areas?

Circle the number under your answer.	Not at all	Several days	More than half the days	Nearly every day
1. I've been interested in doing things.	0	1	3	5
2. I've felt optimistic, excited, and hopeful.	0	1	3	5
3. I've slept well and woken up feeling rested.	0	1	3	5
4. I've had lots of energy.	0	1	3	5
5. I've been able to focus on tasks and use self-discipline.	0	1	3	5
6. I've stayed healthy, eaten well, exercised, and had fun.	0	1	3	5
7. I've felt good about my relationships with my family and friends.	0	1	3	5
8. I'm satisfied with my accomplishments at home, work, or school.	0	1	3	5
9. I'm comfortable with my financial situation.	0	1	3	5
10. I feel good about the spiritual base of my life.	0	1	3	5
11. I'm satisfied with the direction of my life.	0	1	3	5
12. I'm fulfilled, with a sense of well-being and peace of mind.	0	1	3	5

Column Totals: _____   _____   _____   _____

Total Score: _____

DAY TWO   DATE: _____

On day one, you started becoming physically calmer and gaining mental clarity as you came to your senses. Maybe it lasted for a while, or maybe it was brief. When you made the map the second time, what pulled you away from hearing any background sounds, feeling the pen, and seeing the ink go onto the paper? Yes, it was your thoughts. Your mind naturally makes thoughts, both positive and negative. You will never get rid of the negative thoughts. In fact, trying to get rid of them only makes things worse. When you push them away, you give them energy. The I-System takes your natural negative thoughts, makes your body become tense, and closes you off from your senses.

When thoughts arise, it helps to label them using a mind-body bridging tool called *thought labeling*. For example, when you're in the shower and the thought *I'll never get through the day* pops into your mind, say to yourself, *I am having the thought "I'll never get through the day,"* return to your showering, and sense the water on your body and the sounds in the shower. Thought labeling lets you see that a thought is *just a thought*. This keeps the I-System from spinning stories that create mind clutter, distress your body, and numb your senses. You are now breaking the vicious cycle of negative thoughts. For example, a thirty-year-old woman whose life had gone from one crisis to another reported, "Showering used to be when I reviewed my crisis list, but now it's my calm time. My husband immediately noticed a dramatic improvement in our mornings."

During your day, whenever a thought pulls you away from what you are doing, label that thought and return your awareness to your activity.

What do you notice?

_____

_____

_____

_____

_____

_____

_____

_____

_____

_____

DAY THREE   DATE: _____

Becoming aware of the sounds around you is one of the *bridging awareness practices* you'll learn in this workbook. With these practices, you create a bridge from a life filled with PTSD symptoms (the damaged self) to a life lived at its best (your true self). Building this bridge is easier than you think.

1. There are many sounds in your environment. During the day, stop and listen to any background sounds, like the white noise of the heating or air conditioning system, the wind blowing through the trees, or the hum of the refrigerator or computer. If your thoughts start to spin, gently return your awareness to what you were doing. While focusing on any background sounds, see what happens to your mind and body. Does your mind settle? Is your body more relaxed? What happens?

_____

_____

_____

_____

_____

_____

_____

_____

_____

_____

_____

_____

When the I-System is active, it closes off your senses until all you are aware of is your mind clutter and body tension. It's like putting your hands over your ears to block out sounds. The I-System not only keeps you from hearing the ever-present background sounds, but also keeps you from experiencing your ever-present healing powers. When you use your senses, your I-System calms, letting you deal with your problems with a calm mind and relaxed body so you can heal after your trauma. For example, a twenty-five-year-old man with a life full of intrusive memories and body tension reported, "I don't know what it is about the fan, but when I hear it, I relax!"

Chapter 1—Day Three cont.

2. For most of us, driving can be a stressful experience, especially in traffic jams and construction delays, and around unsafe drivers who believe they're the only ones on the road. When driving, keep the radio, music player, and cell phone off. Note what happens to your body tension as you feel the steering wheel, hear the roar and feel the vibrations of the engine, see the scenery, and pay attention to the road.

   What was it like to drive today?

   _____

   _____

   _____

   _____

   _____

   Many have reported to us that this practice has literally saved their lives.

3. When falling asleep tonight, listen to and focus on background sounds. Feel and rub the sheets with your fingers. See the darkness when your eyes are closed. Be patient and keep returning to your senses. The busy head can never settle the busy head. If you wake up in the middle of the night, label your thoughts; for example, *I'm having the thought "That was a bad nightmare,"* or *I'm having the thought "I'll never go back to sleep,"* and then return to your senses. This nighttime practice is essential to your well-being.

   Observations:

   _____

   _____

   _____

   _____

   _____

A Vietnam War veteran with chronic, severe sleep problems told us, "I have an old rottweiler that sleeps on my bedroom floor and a young mutt that sleeps on my bed. Now I just *listen* to the old guy snore and *feel* the fur of the little guy. I haven't slept so well in twenty years!"

You are developing your bridging awareness practices. Remember to keep using the exercises from previous days.

DAY FOUR   DATE: _____

You've touched hundreds of things today. Were you aware of how it felt under your fingertips when you touched your shoes, socks, shirt, keys, fork, watch, paper, or computer? Were you aware of your senses when you touched your child or a close friend? Did you sense the coffee cup or water bottle in your hand? Chances are, you didn't. Your I-System has numbed your body, detaching you from your senses. Tuning in to your sense of touch is another bridging awareness practice that quiets your I-System.

During the day, be aware of the sensations under your fingertips as you touch things like glasses, phones, pens, computers, and other objects and surfaces. When you are washing your hands or showering, feel the water touching your skin. Sense what it's like to touch others or be touched. This may take some effort, because the I-System numbs your senses. A forty-five-year-old man with PTSD said, "The walk to my boss's office was always a hell walk for me. Now, I just feel my feet on the floor and listen to the sound of my steps. It's still not pleasant, but it's a whole new experience. My boss even asked me if I'm on new medication." An Iraq War veteran told us that simply rubbing and sensing his thumb against his finger calmed him down enough to prevent him from punching someone.

Note what you touched, how often, and the sensations you felt throughout the day. Do you feel more settled when you are aware of what you are touching? What happened?

_____

_____

_____

_____

_____

_____

_____

A college student shared this: "I clean houses to pay my tuition. I was always resentful and upset, but now when I clean houses, I feel the vacuum in my hand, smell the cleaner, and see the water move in the sink. Now I don't need to go jogging or be on top of a mountain to feel good about myself!"

You are still developing your bridging awareness practices. Remember to also use the practices from previous days.

DAY FIVE   DATE: _____

The next bridging awareness practice uses the sense of sight, and it's actually hard. The I-System makes up stories that cause us to grasp at certain images and reject others. When you use one or more of your senses, the I-System calms down. When we come to our senses, our awareness expands and we actually see what's out there. When you look at a sunset or even a speck of dust on the floor, does your busy head let you see its colors, shapes, and uniqueness? Probably not for long. Take a look at your next meal. When your food is in front of you, really look at it before you eat it. What textures are there? What are the shapes? What color is it?

How often do you just look at someone's facial features? A man with a history of losing his temper shared this: "When my wife used that high-pitched voice to criticize me, I would lose it. Now I look at her face, watch her lips move, and notice her facial expression; and for some reason, I feel close to her. Even her high-pitched voice is starting to have a sweetness to it."

Pay attention today to what you see when you look at scenery and objects. Notice their colors, shapes, and forms. When you really see what's out there, your I-System rests. Observe others' facial expressions, and if you get a thought, label it, "just a thought," and gently return to whatever you were doing.

Observations:

_____

_____

_____

_____

_____

_____

_____

_____

_____

You are continuing to develop your bridging awareness practices. Remember to also use the practices from previous days.

DAY SIX   DATE: _____

Throughout the day, use your bridging awareness practices (come to your senses) to bust stress and stay relaxed and focused. When thoughts pull you away from your activities, label them. For example, a veteran of the war in Afghanistan shared that she became angry and frustrated whenever her coworkers seemed to spend too much time on breaks, talk too much, or move too slowly. She had quit two jobs and was about to quit this one when she learned about mind-body bridging. Now when she notices the thought *My coworkers are taking too much time on breaks*, she labels it by saying to herself, *I am having the thought "My coworkers are taking too much time on breaks."* She then uses her senses by feeling her heel in her shoe, seeing her coworkers' movement, and listening to the air conditioner. Her body relaxes, and she goes on with her duties as a nurse. Though still disappointed with her coworkers, she is no longer frustrated or furious.

List any stressful situations you had today. What practices did you use? Did you use thought labeling? What happened?

Stress	Awareness Practices	Thought Labeling	What Happened?

You are still developing your bridging awareness practices. Remember to also use the practices from previous days.

DAY SEVEN   DATE: _____

These assignments aren't just exercises; they are your daily life. You may ask yourself, *Can listening to background sounds, feeling my feet on the ground, and being aware of what I touch really help my PTSD symptoms? Can it really be so simple?* If you keep applying these exercises, every cell of your body will shout yes!

One rainy evening, Jeff, a Vietnam War veteran with long-standing PTSD, was taking care of his grandchildren. He got an emergency call that his father had just had a severe heart attack and he needed to get to the hospital right away. Jeff hated driving in heavy rain (especially at night), because it reminded him of the torrential rains in Vietnam. Feeling that he had no choice, he loaded the grandkids in the car and started driving. His mind began filling with racing thoughts, and the pressure in his chest made it difficult to breathe. Using his mind-body bridging practices, he began to actually feel the steering wheel in his hands, which helped him relax his grip. He listened to the sound of the engine, felt the road vibrations, and paid attention to the road. At the end of his trip, even the sound of the rain didn't agitate him. He told us, "My bridging awareness practices saved my life and my grandchildren's."

Use all of your bridging awareness practices and thought labeling in your daily life. Throughout the day, be aware of your activities. For example, feel your foot as it touches the ground, sense your fingertips on the computer keys, hear the hum of the computer, feel the pressure on your behind as you sit, feel the fork in your hand, look at your food, and be aware of how the broom moves the dust when you sweep.

Next write what bridging awareness practices you used, when they worked, and when they didn't.

1. What bridging awareness practices did you use? Be specific.

_____

_____

_____

_____

_____

_____

_____

_____

_____

_____

Chapter 1—Day Seven cont.

2. When did your bridging awareness practices work?

_____

_____

_____

_____

_____

_____

3. When did your bridging awareness practices *not* work?

_____

_____

_____

_____

_____

_____

4. When you were able to "pull your hands from your ears" by quieting your I-System, was it a little easier to deal with your day and your symptoms? How?

_____

_____

_____

_____

You are still developing your bridging awareness practices. Remember to also use the practices from previous days.

The following scale lets you see how well you are using this week's activities in your daily life.

MBB WEEKLY EVALUATION SCALE
SELF-DISCOVERY AND SELF-HEALING OF PTSD

Date: _____

During the past week, how did you do with these practices? Check the description that best matches your practice: hardly ever, occasionally, usually, or almost always.

How frequently did you…	Hardly Ever	Occasionally	Usually	Almost Always
Listen to background sounds?				
Sense the sensations of your fingers when holding your water bottle, coffee cup, cold glass of water, or soda can?				
Sense the sensations of your fingers when you touch things?				
Experience pressure on your feet when you walk?				
Experience pressure on your behind as you sat?				
Feel the steering wheel, hear the roar of the car engine, and pay attention to the road when you were driving?				
Hear the water going down the drain and experience it on your body when you were showering or washing your hands?				
Become keenly aware of everyday activities like making the bed, eating, brushing your teeth, and lifting?				
Become aware of your body sensations when you touched others?				
Become keenly aware of others' facial expressions?				
Use bridging practices to help you relax and stay focused at home and at work?				
Use bridging practices to help you sleep?				
Use bridging practices to bust stress or melt misery?				
Sense that you are connected to your own wellspring of healing, goodness, and wisdom?				

List two new things you've noticed about your life since starting your mind-body bridging practice:

_____

_____

CHAPTER 2

IMPROVE EVERYDAY LIFE BY MELTING AWAY YOUR TENSION

You may have noticed that we haven't talked about your trauma experiences or focused on your most troubling PTSD symptoms. We are not underestimating the significance of your trauma. We know it affects every aspect of your life. For now, let's focus on the role the I-System plays in keeping your PTSD going. The truth is that right here, right now, you are healing yourself from PTSD when your I-System is resting.

In the first chapter we focused on your foundation tools (bridging awareness practices and thought labeling), and you learned that using your senses and labeling your thoughts gives you new information about yourself and the world around you. You learned to use those tools to quiet your overactive I-System. In this chapter, you will learn to use tools that *prevent* the I-System from getting activated. You will move from a reactive state to a proactive state.

Let's talk about how the I-System works. Many different systems regulate our bodies. For instance, we have a temperature regulation system that keeps our body temperature around 98.6 degrees Fahrenheit. If our temperature goes up, we sweat, and if it goes down, we shiver, as our system tries to get back to the body's normal temperature. Similarly, we all have an I-System. It works like our temperature regulation system, but instead of an ideal temperature, the I-System has an "ideal picture" of how the world should be. Each moment, both systems sense whether they are meeting their requirements. When the temperature regulation system requirement is not fulfilled, we shiver or sweat. When the I-System requirements are not fulfilled, we have body tension, mind clutter, and trouble doing what we need to do.

The natural state of the I-System is to rest. It's activated only by requirements. *Requirements* are rules your I-System has about how you and the world should be at any moment (for example, *My spouse should be more understanding, People shouldn't drive twenty-five miles per hour in a forty-five-mile-per-hour zone*). Noticing your I-System's requirements is the first step to keeping everyday events from negatively affecting you. *Any* thought becomes a requirement when it triggers the I-System into action; for example, *It shouldn't rain* is a thought, but when the I-System makes it a requirement, that thought creates body tension, like a tight back, and may bring up past memories, like sloshing through the Vietnam battlefields. It's not what the thought is about (the content), but what happens to the thought, that makes it a requirement. When the I-System makes it a requirement, the thought brings up memories that are full of stories and body tension. You experience the rain through that filter and go through your day living in the past. When your I-System is resting and doesn't make a thought into a requirement, your mind is clear and your body relaxed. You see the rain as just rain and think it's just another rainy day.

The determining factor is whether or not your I-System is active. For example, when you're driving, someone recklessly cuts in front of you. You might think, *How could he cut in front of me? He should know better; he's reckless.* Your hands clench around the steering wheel, you breathe faster, your face gets red, and your shoulders go up. You have the telltale signs of an active I-System that's been triggered by the requirement *No one should recklessly cut in front of me.* Everyone thinks others should drive safely. When the I-System takes control of the thought, *No one should recklessly cut in front of me*, it becomes a requirement. Your blood pressure and stress level rise, impairing your ability to drive safely. Even after the careless driver has turned off the freeway, your mind remains cluttered with thoughts, and your body is still tense. Isn't it bad enough that a reckless driver has nearly caused an accident? Your I-System pours salt on the wound by continuing to spin your thoughts and tense your body. Your day could be ruined, or even worse, your distress could cause you to have an accident later. It's important to notice that whenever the I-System captures a natural thought and makes it into a requirement, you become a victim of circumstances. Using bridging awareness tools and thought labeling helps you prevent your I-System from turning events into destructive experiences. Recognizing requirements is the most important tool you'll learn.

In this chapter, you will map your I-System requirements. Remember, maps are short writing exercises that take only a few minutes. Like doodles, they're little snapshots of your thoughts and body tension. Every map you make increases your awareness of your requirements, reduces your I-System's control, and increases your personal power.

DAY ONE   DATE: _____

1. Throughout the day, look out for the telltale signs of an overactive I-System: body tension, mind clutter, and difficulty doing something. See if you can quiet your I-System by using bridging awareness practices and thought labeling, and returning your awareness to your activity.

   a. What happened when your I-System was overactive?

Situation	Body Tension	Mind Clutter	How You Acted

   b. How often was your I-System overactive today? _____

   c. Describe what happened today when you rested your I-System using mind-body bridging tools (bridging awareness practices and thought labeling).

Situation	Body Tension	Mind-Body Bridging Tools	How You Acted

   d. When you quieted your I-System, was your mind clearer? Yes _____ No _____

Chapter 2—Day One cont.

2. Do a How the World Should Be map (see the following sample map). Take a few minutes to scatter around the oval any thoughts you have about how your everyday world should be, (for example, *Others should be kind and appropriate* or *I shouldn't make any mistakes*). Be specific, working quickly without editing your thoughts.

MAP: HOW THE WORLD SHOULD BE

HOW THE
WORLD SHOULD BE

Chapter 2—Day One cont.

SAMPLE MAP: HOW THE WORLD SHOULD BE

Chris should show
me respect.

People shouldn't
talk too much.

There should be peace
in the world.

I shouldn't be tense.

Everyone should drive
safely.

HOW THE
WORLD SHOULD BE

My son should
always behave.

Lisa should be more
compassionate.

I shouldn't make
mistakes.

People shouldn't
stare at me.

Chapter 2—Day One cont.

a. Do you think everything on your map will happen? Yes _____ No _____

b. In this chart, write each thought and your body tension when you realized it might not happen.

"How the World Should Be" Thought	Body Tension and Location	✓
Example 1: Chris should show me respect	Tight fist, tense jaw	✓
Example 2: There should be peace in the world.	Minimal body tension	

c. The body tension you listed is a sign that the thought is a requirement and has activated your I-System. Place a check mark in the third column to indicate that the particular thought is a requirement.

Your I-System can capture your thoughts about how the world should be. When you experience the reality that how you think things should be isn't how things happen, your body tenses and your mind gets cluttered, limiting how you live your life. Remember, thoughts that trigger your I-System are requirements. In the previous example, take the thought *Chris should show me respect*. When you have thoughts about how Chris is being disrespectful, your body tension might be tight fists and a tense jaw, like in the example. So your requirement would be *Chris should show me respect*. For the other thought listed as an example, *There should be peace in the world*, you would have minimal body tension when reality doesn't match that thought. In that case, your I-System isn't triggered, so the thought *There should be peace in the world* isn't a requirement. It doesn't mean you won't work toward having a peaceful world, but it does mean you can do so with a calm body and clear mind.

Chapter 2—Day One cont.

3. Now you'll use the bridging awareness practices you learned in chapter 1 and do a How the World Should Be map again. Before you start writing, listen to any background sounds, experience your body's pressure on your seat, sense your feet on the floor, and feel the pen in your hand. Once you feel settled, keep feeling the pen in your hand and start writing about how the world should be. Watch the ink go onto the paper, and listen to any background sounds. For the next few minutes, jot whatever comes to mind about how the world should be.

```
                    ⬭
               HOW THE
           WORLD SHOULD BE
                    ⬭
```

a. What are the differences between this map and the map in exercise 1?

_____

_____

_____

_____

b. Do you see that you can face the world as it is, without the pressure and distortion of your I-System that's shown on the previous map you made?

_____

_____

_____

When a situation comes up in your life (*Chris doesn't show me respect*), tune in to your senses and you'll no longer have an overactive I-System adding mind clutter and body tension. You can now face that situation with a ready and relaxed mind and body.

DAY TWO   DATE: _____

Whenever you have body tension and mind clutter, it's a sign that one of your I-System's requirements is not being fulfilled. This exercise is about increasing your awareness of your requirements, and then using bridging awareness practices and thought labeling to reduce your I-System's activity. Recognizing requirements is another mind-body bridging tool. Once you identify a requirement, you'll be clearer about the situation.

A twenty-two-year-old Iraq War combat veteran waits in a government office for an appointment to discuss his Veterans Administration benefits. After checking in and waiting ten minutes, he becomes tense. Five minutes later, he storms out of the office, swearing to himself. He realizes his distress comes from the thought *The VA doesn't care about me!* Later he decides he's too pissed off to go through the process of applying for benefits. Fortunately, this vet enters a mind-body bridging group, where he's able to identify his requirement (*The VA should care about me*) and develop a strong bridging awareness practice. Several weeks later, he decides to go back to the benefits office. After checking in and waiting ten minutes, he notices his chest tightening, fists clenching, and thoughts spinning, and recognizes these as signs of his overactive I-System. Then, using his newly learned bridging awareness practices, he feels the fabric on the chair and his feet on the floor, and hears the hum of the air conditioner. He starts relaxing a little, and clearly sees his I-System's requirement, *They shouldn't keep me waiting*. After ten more minutes, he is called in and applies for his benefits. Is he cured of his symptoms? No! But he *is* developing tools that are greatly improving the quality of his life. As he puts it, "I'm starting to realize that though anyone can kick my tires, my I-System is the only thing that can let the air out of them."

Be on the lookout for your requirements during the day. Notice your own earliest indicators of an overactive I-System. For example, maybe you start to raise your shoulders, your toes curl, you feel overwhelmed, you grip your golf club too hard, you feel a pain in your neck, you stop hearing the fan, or you slump in your chair. Once you notice a sign, see if you can find the requirement that activated your I-System. When you identify your requirement, you have more control over what's upsetting you. Remember, it's not the other person's behavior that activates your I-System; it's your own requirement.

Next, list what requirements you observed today and what happened when you used bridging awareness practices and thought labeling.

Chapter 2—Day Two cont.

1. List the requirements you observed today:

2. Did your bridging awareness practices and thought labeling put you more in control when you used them? What happened?

DAY THREE   DATE: _____

A *trigger* is an event or thought that violates a requirement that, in turn, activates your I-System. Any event or thought is a trigger if, and *only* if, that event or thought violates a requirement. Every coin has two sides, and even when flipped, it's still the same coin. Triggers and requirements are the same way. When you become aware of a trigger, it's important to realize that it points you to the requirement (the other side of the coin). Remember, it's not the event itself that activates the I-System; it's your requirement about that event.

1. Today, observe what triggered your I-System, and list the behaviors or events and your body tension.

Trigger Behavior or Event	Body Tension and Location
Example 1: A guy drove twenty in a forty-mile-per-hour zone.	*Jaw tight, clenched fist*
Example 2: I did it wrong.	*Pressure in chest, foot tapping*

Your body tension is your *signal* that your I-System has been activated. Next, note the thoughts and stories you weave about the trigger behavior or event.

_____

_____

_____

_____

Chapter 2—Day Three cont.

2. Do a Triggers map by jotting down what triggered your I-System, such as how others behave or demands you make of yourself (for example, *Terry broke his promise*, *I did it wrong*, or *Ann doesn't respect me*).

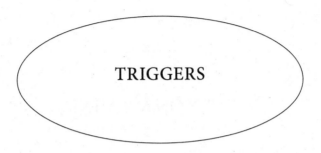

3. From your Triggers map, write down your body tension, triggers, and requirements. Mind-body mapping is always about *your* I-System requirements, not someone else's behavior. Remember that the trigger points to your requirement.

Body Tension	Trigger	Requirement
Tight shoulders	Terry broke his promise.	Terry shouldn't break his promise.

How many requirements did you identify?

DAY FOUR   DATE: _____

1. Whenever it's hard to find the underlying requirements, it's helpful to do a What's on My Mind map. Take a couple of minutes to write whatever pops into your mind around the following oval. Work quickly, without editing your thoughts.

WHAT'S ON MY MIND

   a. Is your mind cluttered or clear?

   _____

   b. Is your body tense or relaxed? Describe your body tension:

   _____

   _____

   This is a momentary snapshot of what's on your mind. Notice which thoughts are connected to body tension (for example, *My life was ruined when I was sexually abused, The bomb's explosion ruined my life, My car needs work*). Recognize the requirement in the item (*I should not have been sexually abused, I should not have been hurt, My car shouldn't be broken*).

   c. What are your requirements?

   _____

   _____

   _____

   _____

Chapter 2—Day Four cont.

2. Do this map again, this time using bridging awareness practices. Before you start writing, listen to any background sounds, feel your body's pressure on your seat, sense your feet on the floor, and feel the pen in your hand. Once you feel settled, keep feeling the pen in your hand, and start writing. Watch the ink go onto the paper, and listen to any background sounds. For the next few minutes, jot whatever thoughts pop into your mind.

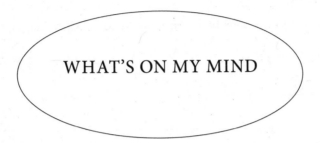

Observe the differences between the two maps:

_____

_____

Remember, thought labeling helps. For example, if you have the thought *I ruined my life*, say to yourself, *I'm having the thought "I ruined my life."* What's ruining your life right here, right now, isn't the bomb (or the abuse), but the thoughts your I-System has spun about the bomb (the abuse). You don't have to fix your thoughts, push them away, or force any changes. During the day, being aware that this thought is just a thought is all it takes; then you can return your awareness to the task at hand.

Mind-body bridging is an ongoing practice. When you use bridging awareness practices (use your senses) and thought labeling, you gain the ability to live every aspect of your life with a calm I-System (your true self). The only question you need to answer is *who* is living your life, your I-System or your true self?

DAY FIVE   DATE: _____

1. Throughout the day, be aware of your body tension. Although the I-System generates body tension and impairs how you live your life, it isn't your enemy any more than a friend who is giving you important information. Awareness of the early signs of body tension lets you know when you are heading the wrong direction. Use it like a compass (figure 2.1). When you recognize that the I-System is on, and you use your mind-body bridging tools to quiet its commotion, it becomes a friend. You are *befriending your I-System*.

    a. When were you able to use your body tension as a compass? What happened?

    _____

    _____

    _____

    _____

    b. When were you *unable* to use your body tension as a compass? What happened?

    _____

    _____

    _____

    _____

    c. Does this compass help you find requirements? How?

    _____

    _____

    When your body is tense and your mind cluttered, your I-System is in the driver's seat. To quiet your I-System, note that it's your requirement, not the situation, that's causing your distress. Next, listen to any background sounds, sense whatever you're touching, and fully return your awareness to what you were doing.

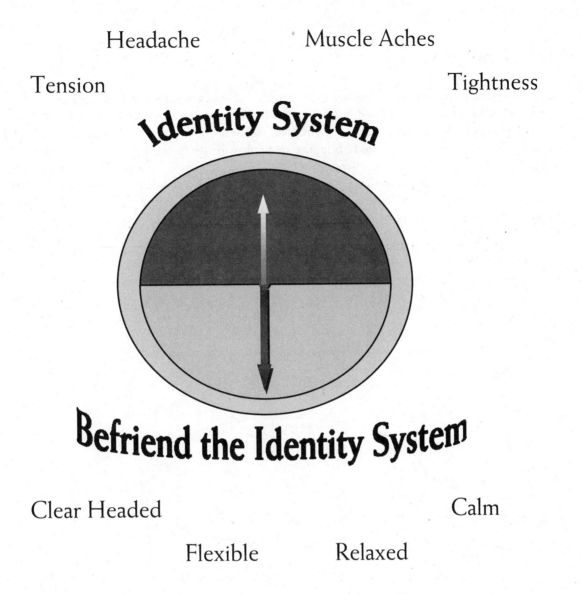

Figure 2.1   Body Sensation Compass

A migratory bird's internal compass tells it when it's veering off course on its way home in the spring. When you befriend your I-System, it becomes your compass, letting you know when you are off course. Your awareness is all it takes, because when your I-System is calm, your natural functioning lets you effectively navigate daily activities, and even any crisis.

Chapter 2—Day Five cont.

2. Do a Problem map. You may be saying to yourself, *I did Problem maps last week; why do I have to do them again?* Great question! It's a different day, with different problems and different maps. Mapping gives you insight into what's happening right here, right now, so each map is a journey of self-discovery. Mapping is a strong mind-body bridging tool you will use to recognize your requirements and quiet your I-System. So let's get started.

   Write a current problem in the center of the oval. Next, take a couple of minutes to scatter around the oval any thoughts that come to mind. Work quickly, without editing your thoughts. List your body tensions at the bottom of the map.

PROBLEM MAP

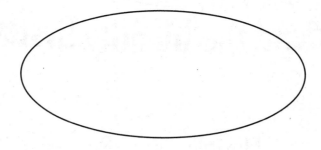

Body Tension:

_____

_____

Chapter 2—Day Five cont.

A woman with both PTSD and alcoholism did a map in a group session. She was scheduled to go to court for her third DUI the next day. She had only a few items on her map. One of her listed thoughts was *Going to court tomorrow*, but she had listed no body tension. She shared that she felt detached and numb, until the group asked her what might happen in court. Her body then tensed, and she became tearful, meaning that she did have an underlying requirement. Doing another Problem map made her aware of her *main* requirement: *The judge should be lenient.*

What does your map say about how you are approaching your problem?

a.   Is your mind cluttered or clear?

_____

b.   Is your body tense or relaxed?

_____

c.   What are your requirements?

_____

_____

_____

_____

_____

_____

_____

If your map has minimal signs of an overactive I-System, it may be that you have no requirements, but that's quite unlikely at this early stage of your practice. What's more likely happening is that your overactive I-System is closing you off, shutting down your normal body sensations.

To find out if that's the case, get out a blank piece of paper and do another map. Put an important thought like *I'm going to court tomorrow*, which brought up no body tension, in the oval. Consider that thought to see what comes to mind and write your thoughts around the oval for three to four minutes.

Many times, your body will then tense, which helps you discover your underlying requirement. Being unaware of your requirement (*The judge should be lenient*) keeps your I-System active. The key to waking up your body and healing yourself is recognizing your requirement. You don't have to force yourself to feel anything. Your natural functioning will let the process take place gently and powerfully.

Chapter 2—Day Five cont.

3. Using the same problem, do another map, this time using your bridging awareness practices. Write the problem in the oval. Before you start writing, listen to any background sounds, feel your body's pressure on your seat, sense your feet on the floor, and feel the pen in your hand. Once you feel settled, keep feeling the pen in your hand, and start writing. Watch the ink go onto the paper, and listen to any background sounds.

PROBLEM MAP WITH BRIDGING

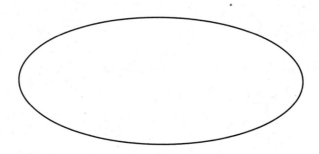

a. Is your mind cluttered or clear?

_____

b. Is your body tense or relaxed?

_____

c. Observe the differences between the two maps:

   i. Are you clearer about your problem? Yes _____ No _____

   ii. In this mind-body state, how would you approach your problem?

_____

_____

   iii. In this mind-body state, do you recognize your ability to heal yourself? Yes _____ No _____

DAY SIX   DATE: _____

1. Throughout the day, observe how your day is going. How do you see the results of mind-body bridging in your daily life?

_____

_____

_____

_____

_____

_____

List any situations where mind-body bridging isn't working. Be specific, and see if you can recognize the requirement responsible for your distress.

Problem Areas	Requirements

Chapter 2—Day Six cont.

2. Do a Problem map. Start by choosing the most stressful problem from the previous list. Write it in the oval in the center of the paper. Next, take a couple of minutes to scatter around the oval any thoughts that come to mind. Work quickly, without editing your thoughts. The mind produces hundreds of thoughts each minute. The more open you are to how your mind works, the more insight you gain. Thoughts like *This is a stupid exercise, This book can't help me,* and *I know enough now to do the map in my head* are perfect to write. Describe your body tension at the bottom of the map.

PROBLEM MAP

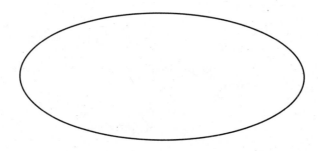

Body Tension:

_____

_____

    a. Is your mind cluttered or clear?

_____

    b. Is your body tense or relaxed?

_____

    c. With the amount of body tension and mind clutter on your map, would your ability to heal yourself be limited? Yes _____ No _____

    d. What requirements did you recognize on this map?

_____

_____

3. Do the same map, this time using your bridging awareness practices. Write the problem in the oval. Before you start writing, listen to any background sounds, feel your body's pressure on your seat, sense your feet on the floor, and feel the pen in your hand. Once you feel settled, keep feeling the pen in your hand, and start writing. Watch the ink go onto the paper, and listen to any background sounds.

PROBLEM MAP WITH BRIDGING

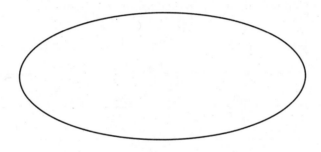

a. Is your mind cluttered or clear?

_____

b. Is your body tense or relaxed?

_____

c. Observe the differences between the two maps:

   i. Are you clearer about your problem? Yes _____ No _____

   ii. In this mind-body state, how would you approach your problem?

_____

_____

d. In this mind-body state, do you recognize your ability to heal yourself?
Yes _____ No _____

DAY SEVEN   DATE: _____

A thirty-year-old woman with PTSD from repeated childhood sexual abuse shared her progress with her women's group: "My Problem maps had *My teenage son's drinking*, *Unpaid bills*, and *My boss from hell*. I believed they were all causing my distress. When I did the maps again using my bridging awareness practices, I realized it wasn't my *problems* but my *requirements* about them that caused my distress. The bridging map gave me a glimpse of who I really am. I began noticing the trees in my yard, the blue color on my walls, and the cool air on my face. I even noticed my days getting easier." She hesitated and asked the group if it was okay to talk about something personal. After getting the go-ahead, she said, "I used to service my husband sexually just because he's such a good guy, but yesterday I had an orgasm with him for the first time." Every woman in the room felt her eyes well with tears.

Mind-body bridging has two parts: the first consists of your bridging awareness practices and thought labeling, and the second is befriending your I-System. You befriend your I-System by using tools like mapping, and recognizing and defusing your requirements.

Today, start using your mind-body bridging practices in your daily life.

1. What happened?

_____

_____

_____

_____

2. What requirements did you recognize?

_____

_____

_____

_____

3. How did mind-body bridging practices help?

_____

_____

_____

_____

MBB WEEKLY EVALUATION SCALE
IMPROVE EVERYDAY LIFE BY MELTING AWAY YOUR TENSION

Date: _____

During the past week, how did you do with these practices? Check the description that best matches your practice: hardly ever, occasionally, usually, or almost always.

How frequently do you...	Hardly Ever	Occasionally	Usually	Almost Always
Locate and recognize body sensations as a sign of an overactive I-System?				
Recognize the destructive effects your I-System has on your life?				
Recognize that an overactive I-System underlies your problems?				
Recognize your requirements?				
Catch yourself drifting away from the present moment?				
Use bridging awareness practices to quiet your I-System and improve the quality of your life?				
Come to appreciate your life in a different light?				
Do a daily mind-body bridging map?				

1. How do things look when your I-System is overactive?

   _____

   _____

2. How do things look when you are bridging and your I-System is at rest?

   _____

   _____

3. What's the most important benefit of doing mind-body bridging maps?

   _____

   _____

BREAK THE TYRANNY OF
NEGATIVE THOUGHTS

PTSD is full of recurring, disturbing, and intrusive thoughts, many of which become negative *self-beliefs*, beliefs you have about yourself. Did you know that from the neuroscience viewpoint, a thought is just a secretion, a droplet of a chemical where two brain cells connect (synapse)? Did you know that psychologists and others studying the mind sometimes call thoughts *mind facts*? These mind facts are organized, stored, and used as needed to fulfill adapt to any situation. The I-System captures certain thoughts and gets stuck on them. This keeps the I-System "on" and the true self "off." Because the true self is in charge of healing, you can't heal while this is happening, leaving you feeling discouraged and damaged. Mind-body bridging practices quiet the I-System, letting your ability to heal yourself resume on its own.

Now, what do we do about those recurring, disturbing, and intrusive negative thoughts? You already know that pushing them away only gives them more energy. For example, try not to think of a red balloon. What are you thinking of? A red balloon! Many books are available that support using positive affirmations to deal with negative thoughts. We have all tried to fix ourselves with positive affirmations, but when we stop, the negative thoughts come back with a vengeance. So the question remains: what do we do with the negative, troubling thoughts?

Let's begin by looking at how the mind works. If we have the thought *high*, there must be a *low*; if we think *good*, there must be a *bad*, and the same follows for *happy* and *sad*, *sick* and *well*, and *young* and *old*. We see that the mind works with both positive and negative thoughts. The only time we will get rid of our negative thoughts is when we're brain dead. This means that if you were in a terminal condition and your EEG suddenly flatlined, your physician might say to herself, *Wow! He finally got rid of his negative thoughts*. With this information, let's see if we can find the right answer to our question.

Our naturally functioning true self creates harmony and balance with both sides of opposite thoughts. For instance, being sick and being well are both conditions of the mind-body. Your true self deals appropriately with each. But the I-System has a totally different approach. The I-System has a part (subsystem) called the *depressor*. The depressor works by taking your negative thoughts and self-talk (things you say to yourself), and creating body tension and mind clutter. It takes a negative thought like *I'm a loser*, *I can't do it*, *I'll never be the same*, *I'm no good*, or *I'm stained*, and weaves a story about that thought, embedding the negativity into every cell of your body. You are left seeing yourself as incomplete, damaged, or broken and you have a story to prove it! This state is known as the *damaged self*.

The original question, *What do I do about my negative thought?* now becomes *What do I do about my depressor?* That's what this chapter is all about.

DAY ONE   DATE: _____

The depressor is the doom and gloom of your I-System, using negative self-talk to reinforce the damaged self. Today you'll begin to recognize your negative self-talk.

1. Throughout the day, notice and log your negative self-talk. Note the nature (such as sharp, cramping, painful, heavy, or tense), location, and intensity of any body tension that comes with it.

Negative Self-Talk	Body Tension

2. Do a Depressor map. Around the following oval, scatter your negative self-talk and any thoughts you have when you're bummed out. (See the sample map on the next page.) Write as much as you can for a couple of minutes. List your body tensions at the bottom of the map.

DEPRESSOR

Body Tension:

_____

_____

What's your behavior like when your depressor is active?

_____

_____

_____

_____

The thoughts on your map are natural thoughts that happen to be negative. The depressor works by grabbing a negative thought and embedding the negativity in your body. The resulting distress you feel starts the vicious cycle as more negative thoughts follow. This creates a heavy burden that affects how you live your life. Seeing how the depressor works breaks this vicious cycle.

Chapter 3—Day One cont.

SAMPLE DEPRESSOR MAP

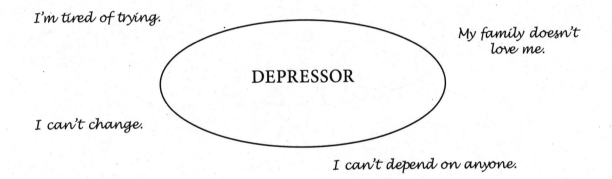

I can't control my life.

I've lost hope.

I'm no good.

I'm tired of trying.

My family doesn't love me.

DEPRESSOR

I can't change.

I can't depend on anyone.

I'm afraid to feel anything.

Body Tension:

clenched jaw, tight shoulders, rumbling stomach, painful neck, heavy body

3. Let's see how your depressor works. From the map you made in step 2, take the thought that creates a lot of body tension and disturbs you the most (for example, *My life is useless* or *I can't do anything right*), and write it in the following oval. Now, scatter around the oval any thoughts that come to mind. Use phrases or complete sentences like *I can't keep a job* or *I was fine before*. List your body tensions at the bottom of the map.

TROUBLING THOUGHT FROM MY DEPRESSOR MAP

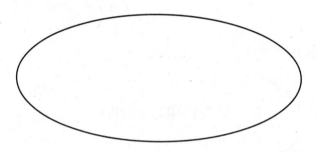

Body Tension:

_____

_____

The map you just did holds the key to controlling your depressor. All the thoughts on your map are spun into stories (true or not) by your I-System. Just think about the stories that come to mind about your negative thoughts. These are called *storylines*. It's very important to recognize and become aware of their power. Storylines are the link between any negative thought that pops into your mind and the mind-body distress you experienced on the last two maps. The I-System's spinning storyline takes a natural negative thought and embeds the negativity into every cell of your body, thereby making a mind-body connection. Storylines keep the I-System going, taking you away from the present moment and keeping you from living your life at its best. Without the depressor's storylines, negative thoughts can not cause any distress.

Chapter 3—Day One cont.

Frank lost his left leg in Iraq. He has a relatively well-functioning prosthesis. Often when he woke up in the morning, he thought, *I'm an amputee*, and then wove negative stories about what he couldn't do, his discomfort, the problem, and so on. By the time he got up to go to the bathroom, his mind and body were already distressed. He blamed his distress on his combat injury and created more storylines about being unable to live his life as he had before the war. Several weeks after starting a mind-body bridging group, he reported, "I sometimes still wake up with the thought *I'm an amputee*, but now I say to myself, *I am having the thought "I'm an amputee," so what else is new?* I then make my way to the bathroom, and if I start to weave a storyline, I just become aware of it while listening to the fan's humming, feeling the pressure on my right foot, and sensing my body's movement. By the time I get to the bathroom, I'm no longer filled with tension and resentment. I don't even need to tell myself positive stories about how I'm a survivor. What I found for myself, by myself, was that it wasn't my war trauma that disabled me in the morning; it was my storylines. My depressor used to make me feel damaged by filling my mind and body with negatives. Now even though I still have only one leg, I'm no longer damaged!"

Another powerful tool is *storyline awareness*. You don't need to push the story away; you just need to be aware of it. Your awareness melts the storyline. Do this exercise: Start mulling over one of your most powerful storylines and try to keep it going. Now, be aware of the background sounds and observe how your storyline unfolds. Is it running out of gas? Do you see how powerful your awareness is? What do you notice?

_____

_____

_____

_____

Look back at the items on your Depressor map and consider each one. See if you can find additional storylines. When spun by your I-System, storylines aren't just stories; they have a direct physical effect on your body and try to create your reality. By using your storyline awareness tool (just being aware of the storyline) during the day, you'll see how much of your day storylines swallow up. We have received hundreds of comments from patients who did this practice, such as, "I procrastinate less," "The clock's moving slower," and "I'm getting more done; I now have time for myself."

What do you notice?

_____

_____

_____

_____

DAY TWO　　　　DATE: _____

1.　Throughout the day, notice when your depressor gets you down. Observe your body tension, storylines, and behaviors. Note how your depressor interferes with your natural functioning, making you see yourself as damaged.

　　a.　How do you recognize when your depressor is overactive? *Example: Heavy body, tight feeling in stomach, thoughts that I'm no good*

　　　　_____

　　b.　What's your behavior like? *Example: Become irritable, want to get away from people, eat too much*

　　　　_____

　　c.　How does it interfere with your natural functioning? *Example: Don't make good decisions, am a lousy parent*

　　　　_____

　　d.　Do you experience yourself as damaged? Yes _____ No _____ If yes, how so?

　　　　_____

　　　　_____

　　e.　What were today's storylines? *Example: The thought—My life is too hard; the storyline—I can't get things done, I'm not the person I need to be, Why did this happen to me? I'm too tired to get through the day...*

　　　　_____

　　f.　In what ways are these thoughts and storylines creating who you are?

　　　　_____

　　g.　What are your requirements? *Example: My life should be easier, I should get things done, I should be the person I used to be, This shouldn't have happened to me, I shouldn't be worn out.*

　　　　_____

　　　　_____

　　　　_____

Chapter 3—Day Two cont.

2. Do a Depressor map, scattering your negative self-talk around the paper. Write as much as you can for a couple of minutes. Describe your body tension at the bottom of the map.

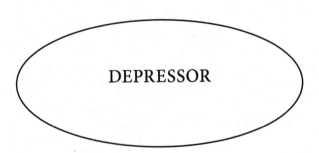

Body Tension:

_____

_____

Did you have thoughts like *I'm a loser*? Remember, labeling your thought lets you see that a thought is just a thought, which keeps you from identifying with the content of that thought. Instead of thinking, *I'm a loser*, say to yourself, *I'm having the thought "I'm a loser."* Can you see that the problem is not the content of your thoughts, but rather the depressor capturing that thought, spinning a storyline, and embedding the negativity in your mind and body? When your awareness prevents the depressor from embedding the negativity of your thoughts into your body, we call it *befriending your depressor*.

Observations:

_____

_____

_____

_____

_____

DAY THREE   DATE: _____

1. Throughout the day, notice what situations (such as being alone, arguing, or making mistakes) and thoughts trigger your depressor. Use your tools: thought labeling, storyline awareness, and bridging awareness practices (using your senses). Can you defuse your depressor's activity and return to what you were doing?

    a. What did you notice today about your situations and the thoughts that activated your depressor?

    _____

    _____

    _____

    _____

    _____

    _____

    _____

    b. In what situations did you use your mind-body bridging tools? How did it go?

    _____

    _____

    _____

    _____

    _____

    _____

    _____

Chapter 3—Day Three cont.

2. Let's do a Mirror map. Find a quiet place and look in a mirror. Before you start writing, really look at yourself for a minute or so. Next, scatter around the oval any thoughts and feelings that come to mind about what you see. Glance back at the mirror several times and keep writing whatever comes to mind.

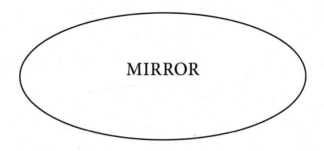

MIRROR

Body Tension:

_____

_____

a. Is your I-System active? Yes _____ No _____

b. Do you recognize your depressor? Yes _____ No _____

c. What are your storylines?

_____

_____

d. Do you recognize that the depressor's activity is making you experience your body as an enemy and making you see yourself as damaged goods? Yes _____ No _____

e. What are your requirements?

_____

_____

_____

Chapter 3—Day Three cont.

3. Do another Mirror map, this time using your bridging awareness practices. Before writing, listen to any background sounds, feel your body's pressure on your seat, sense your feet on the floor, and feel the pen in your hand. Now look in the mirror and keep listening to background sounds. After you feel settled, jot around the oval whatever thoughts pop into your mind. Keep listening to background sounds and feeling the pen in your hand. Watch the ink go onto the paper.

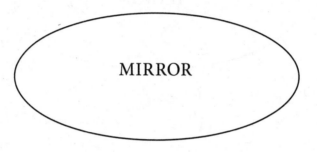

a. How is this map different from your first Mirror map?

_____

_____

_____

_____

_____

b. Do you notice that the same facial features are on both maps? Yes _____ No _____

c. Using mind-body bridging awareness practices, do you have a new level of self-acceptance? Yes _____ No _____

DAY FOUR   DATE: _____

1. Do a How I Got to Be the Way I Am map. Around the oval, write how you got to be the way you are (for example, *My father was never around, I survived repeated abuse, Mom was always there to support me*). Write for three to four minutes. List your body tensions at the bottom of the map. A sample map follows.

⬭ **HOW I GOT TO BE THE WAY I AM**

Body Tension:

_____

_____

a. What storyline themes run through your map?

_____

_____

b. Next describe when and how often you use these storylines—for example, when you feel like a success or failure, when you're sad or happy, or when you're bored or busy.

_____

_____

Whenever your I-System uses stories, the stories keep you from living in the present. No matter what the content, storylines tense your body, limit your awareness, and impair your ability to function. They strengthen your false belief in the damaged self. Being more aware of your storylines lets your I-System rest so that you automatically start seeing yourself as much greater than you thought you were.

Chapter 3—Day Four cont.

SAMPLE MAP: HOW I GOT TO BE THE WAY I AM

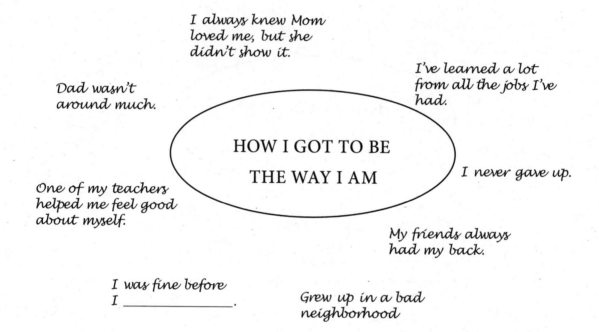

Poor school district

Mom was depressed.

I always knew Mom loved me, but she didn't show it.

Dad wasn't around much.

I've learned a lot from all the jobs I've had.

HOW I GOT TO BE THE WAY I AM

I never gave up.

One of my teachers helped me feel good about myself.

My friends always had my back.

I was fine before I _____.

Grew up in a bad neighborhood

Body Tension:

headache, stiff neck

DAY FIVE   DATE: _____

A twenty-five-year-old combat veteran struggled with our exercises, including mapping. He couldn't see the purpose of these activities, and more important, he didn't get the benefits. To his credit, he kept doing daily maps and, one day, exclaimed, "I found it!" His clinician asked what he had found, and he told this story:

> I was mapping about the strong urge to wash my hands. The items on my initial map were *I'm dirty, Bad, Guilty,* and *Can't do anything until I wash.* I thought my requirement was *I need to have clean hands.* That didn't do me any good. I did map after map. Finally, it popped out. The requirement is *I should have helped my brother this morning when he called about his car problem.*

He went on to explain the sequence of events:

> He called me with car troubles this morning. After ten minutes, I hung up on him. Soon after, that hand-washing urge started up. I didn't pay much attention because the urges weren't new. But later, I started mapping. Then that requirement *I should've helped my brother with his car problem* popped up. I saw [this requirement] and felt released of my need to wash my hands. I got to the bottom of it, which was *not* my being dirty. Now when I need to wash my hands, or even if I feel uncomfortable, after doing a map, I can smile because I can figure out the hidden requirement. It's like finding the last piece of the puzzle. By recognizing my requirements early, I can keep my I-System from activating.

A month later, his ongoing mapping practice helped him find other requirements, greatly relieving many of his PTSD symptoms. As he had mentioned, the first step is to recognize the obvious requirement. Next, by doing the daily assignments, you'll find other requirements that aren't obvious right now (hidden requirements).

During the day, observe how your I-System weaves both positive and negative self-talk into stories. What was the situation? Note the hidden requirement.

Storyline	Situation	Requirement
I'll never get a job, bad economy, I'm no good...	*Out of work*	*I should be employed.*

The negative storylines try to *define* us, and the positive ones try to *confine* us. All storylines lead us into the past, future, or both, taking us away from functioning freely in the present.

DAY SIX   DATE: _____

1. Do a Problem map, using any personal issue that's troubling you. Write the problem in the oval. Next, take a couple of minutes to scatter around the paper any thoughts that come to mind. Work quickly, without editing your thoughts. Describe your body tension at the bottom of the map.

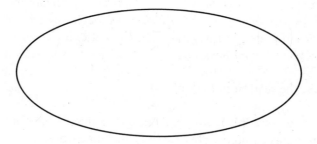

Body Tension:

_____

_____

    a.   Is your mind cluttered or clear?

_____

    b.   Is your body tense or relaxed?

_____

    c.   List your depressors and storylines:

_____

_____

    d.   List your requirements:

_____

_____

    e.   In this mind-body state, how do you act?

_____

Chapter 3—Day Six cont.

2. Now do the map again, this time using your bridging awareness practices. Write the same problem in the oval. Before you continue, listen to background sounds, feel your body's pressure on your seat, sense your feet on the floor, and feel the pen in your hand. Once you feel settled, keep feeling the pen in your hand and start writing. Watch the ink go onto the paper, and listen to background sounds.

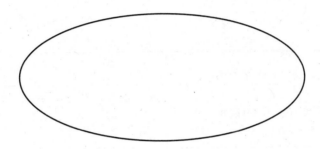

Notice the differences between the two maps:

a. Is your mind cluttered or clear?

_____

b. Is your body tense or relaxed?

_____

c. In this mind-body state, how do you act?

_____

_____

_____

DAY SEVEN   DATE: _____

Today, include all your bridging awareness tools in your activities:

- ◆ Bridging awareness practices

- ◆ Thought labeling

- ◆ Storyline awareness

- ◆ Recognizing and defusing the depressor's activity (befriending the depressor)

- ◆ Recognizing and defusing requirements

1. What happened?

_____

_____

2. How did you recognize your depressor activity?

_____

_____

_____

3. Were you able to defuse the depressor's activity (befriend your depressor)?

_____

_____

4. How did you recognize and defuse your requirements?

_____

_____

_____

5. How did mind-body bridging practices help with your life?

_____

_____

_____

MBB Weekly Evaluation Scale
Break the Tyranny of Negative Thoughts

Date: _____

During the past week, how did you do with these practices? Check the description that best matches your practice: hardly ever, occasionally, usually, or almost always

How frequently do you...	Hardly Ever	Occasionally	Usually	Almost Always
Recognize negative self-talk and body tension as a sign of the depressor?				
Notice that your depressor is running wild and making you feel totally bad (damaged self)?				
Locate body sensations linked to the depressor?				
During the day, experience the beneficial effects of befriending your depressor by staying aware of its activity and using thought labeling?				
Recognize storylines?				
See that the damaged self is from your I-System and is a myth?				
Recognize natural functioning when your I-System is calm?				

List the main body tensions you notice with the depressor:

_____

List the themes of three negative storylines:

_____

_____

List three behaviors that go with the depressor:

_____

_____

What's it like to befriend your depressor and function naturally?

_____

_____

CHAPTER 4

WHY YOUR BEST EFFORTS
SEEM TO GO WRONG

Jim, a twenty-eight-year-old veteran who'd done tours of duty in both Iraq and Afghanistan, had seen a great deal of combat and been discharged two years ago. He kept feeling "revved up," and looked for "edgy," dangerous activities. He sometimes needed to avoid certain social situations. At other times, he was tense, irritable, and frustrated. He thought it weak that he sometimes couldn't "hold it together," which pushed him to try harder to be how he was before going into the service. He pushed his symptoms out of his mind and tried to tell himself everything was normal by being upbeat and making others think he could handle anything, He considered his difficulty adjusting to civilian life to be normal and thought it would get better with time, but his symptoms didn't improve, and his job and marriage held on by a thread.

This chapter focuses on why the feeling of being driven—the "try harder" and "be stronger" attitude—is never enough. For instance, rather than give in to his symptoms, Jim declared war on them. As soon as he saw any sign of helplessness or weakness, he immediately pushed himself to try harder. He came to believe that he was broken because his efforts fell far short of his expectations. Whatever he tried to do, enough was never enough, causing even more mind clutter and body tension. No matter how hard he tried or how well he did, his inner tension never went away. He couldn't "fix" himself.

The *fixer* is the I-System's helper, the depressor's lifelong, faithful partner. The depressor and fixer keep the I-System going and lead to the disruptive mind-body state, the damaged self. Your fixer comes up with overactive thoughts and storylines that focus on how to fix you and the world. The fixer brings a sense of urgency and pressure to your activities, and when it's in play, enough is never enough. Your fixer starts from the false belief that you are damaged, tries to fix you, and works by making you believe it's really helping you. You can recognize the fixer by noticing your increased body tension when the embedded depressor fills your mind with thoughts like *Enough is never enough, Try harder, Do more, Be smarter,* or *Be stronger.* No matter what you accomplish, the depressor says, *Not good enough.*

Jim didn't know his fixer was in the driver's seat. He believed this state of impaired functioning and lack of healing was a "normal" part of his life. His combat experiences activated his I-System, and his PTSD symptoms caused him to experience himself as damaged. Despite Jim's best efforts, his fixer never fixed his damaged self. Remember from the introduction, the damaged self doesn't refer to decreased mental or physical functioning due to injury, illness, trauma, or even your DNA. The damaged self is the mind-body state you're in when your overactive I-System makes you feel incomplete, limited, and damaged, keeping you from healing. The fixer can't fix the damaged self, because the fixer is part of the I-System, the very thing that causes the 'damaged self' state of mind and body.

Using mind-body bridging tools, Jim started recognizing his fixer by noticing his specific body tension and mental pressure. He saw the stress and strain the fixer caused, which was difficult at first, because trying harder, fighting, and overcoming obstacles was part of his nature. But soon, he saw that the need for "fixing" never ended, and felt the extra tension that came with the fixer. He found that for every fixer thought (for example, *Be stronger* or *Be successful*), there was an embedded depressor thought (for example, *I'm weak* or *I'm a failure*). He saw clearly that what motivated him was not success. No matter how many successes he had, the tension never left, and he never found peace of mind or a sense of well-being. During his daily activities, whenever his chest tightened, he realized it was the telltale sign of his depressor and fixer activity. Using his mind-body bridging tools in his everyday life, he drove himself less and accomplished more while reducing his PTSD symptoms. Jim was learning what it was like to function naturally and be free of the disturbances his I-System had caused.

Now it's your turn.

DAY ONE   DATE: _____

1. Throughout the day, notice the signs of your fixer. Remember, you recognize them by noticing body tension and the urgent self-talk (storylines) that make you think you need to fix yourself and the world. When you do an activity, notice any specific body tension, mental pressure, or feeling of being driven.

Activity	Body Tension and Location	Storyline	Fixer Thought
Going to work	Headache, chest pressure	I can't be late again. Why didn't I get up earlier? Bad traffic...	Go through yellow lights; drive faster ✓

Review your log and put a check mark next to fixers that come with strong mental pressure or urgency. See if you can find the different characteristics of body tension (location, type, or both) that come with the fixer.

The fixer may also be involved when you can't seem to resolve an issue. Maybe at night when you're trying to sleep, a situation plays over and over in your mind. Your I-System's fixer is in full gear, trying to figure out how to fix everything, yet interfering with your sleep. Remember to use bridging awareness practices for a good night's sleep.

Chapter 4—Day One cont.

2. Do a Fixer map. Around the oval, jot the thoughts that come up about "How I Am Going to Improve My Life." Work quickly for three to four minutes, without editing your thoughts.

HOW I AM GOING TO
IMPROVE MY LIFE

a. When you look at your overall map, how do you feel?

Calm _____ Tense _____ Overwhelmed _____

The statements on your map may be either fixers or healthy thoughts (from natural functioning) about taking care of yourself and your responsibilities. For all your efforts and good intentions to succeed, it's important to know which of your daily activities the fixer is impairing. One way to do this is to consider each item on your map and figure how much body tension you have when you think about going for this self-improvement goal.

b. Next to each item on your map, note your level of body tension using one of these symbols: Ø for no body tension, + for mild, ++ for moderate, or +++ for severe. It may help to see the sample Fixer map at the end of today's assignments.

   The thoughts that come with body tension are your fixers, and the thoughts with no body tension are from natural functioning. The challenge is telling the difference between the two. Body tension that comes with thoughts means your fixer is active. The fixer also brings a mental urgency, creating extra pressure for you to act. Remember, natural functioning is how you think, feel, see the world, and act when your I-System is calm. When you are functioning naturally, and don't reach a goal, you're naturally disappointed. But when you don't reach a fixer goal, you feel terrible.

Chapter 4—Day One cont.

c. List your fixers from the previous map:

_____

_____

_____

d. List thoughts on the previous map that are from natural functioning:

_____

_____

_____

e. It will help to compare the Depressor map in chapter 3, Day One, to this Fixer map:

    i. Which map has the higher overall energy levels (makes you feel better)? Depressor map _____ Fixer map _____

        Elevated energy levels that come with the fixer—which make you feel better—aren't unusual. This higher endorphin level may keep you from recognizing the fixer, because you feel good about the thoughts. This makes you prone to addictions, risk-taking activities, and overworking when the thoughts are _Drink more alcohol_, _Drive faster than anyone else_, and _Work more_. When active, the fixer impairs your judgment about the effects of your actions.

    ii. Make connections between the items on the Depressor map and the Fixer map:

_____

_____

    iii. Note the differences in location, quality, and intensity of the body tension that comes with the thoughts on the two maps; for example, _My body tension on the Depressor map was located around my gut, and my body felt heavy and unresponsive. On my Fixer map, my body tension is around my chest and head, and there's a jittery feeling._

_____

_____

        The intensity of your body tension and the driving pressure of your storylines are important signs that your fixer is active. Storylines are a sign that your fixer is limiting your ability to deal well with your current activity.

Chapter 4—Day One cont.

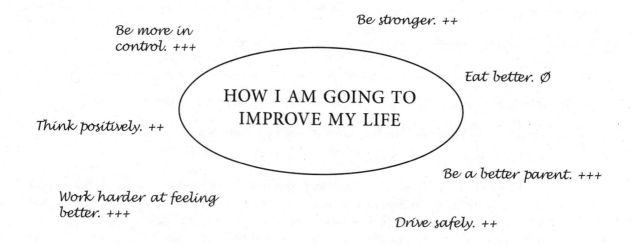

SAMPLE FIXER MAP

Read more books on PTSD. Ø

Be more in control. +++

Be stronger. ++

Eat better. Ø

HOW I AM GOING TO IMPROVE MY LIFE

Think positively. ++

Be a better parent. +++

Work harder at feeling better. +++

Drive safely. ++

Don't depend on anybody. +++

Note the fixers that come with a body tension level of **++** or **+++** when you think about trying to reach self-improvement goals; for example, *Be independent, Don't depend on anybody, Work harder at feeling better, Be a better parent, Be more in control, Be stronger, Think positively,* and *Drive safely.*

Also note any thoughts from natural functioning (without body tension, Ø) when you go for a self-improvement goal; for example, *Read more books on PTSD* or *Eat better.*

DAY TWO   DATE: _____

The fixer's activity takes many forms. For instance, George mows his lawn two to three times a week. He always tried to make it perfect because it is "never good enough." Mary was on an endless merry-go-round, left exhausted from so busily meeting her children's needs. Mike drove himself so hard at work that he needed medicine to lower his blood pressure. Ray tried so hard to be a "good husband" that his wife almost left him. Larry's trauma symptoms so overwhelmed him that he tried to "fix" himself with a bottle of whiskey a day. Tom found driving fast so exciting that it was the thing that made him feel alive. And Ted was always angry.

We have all read about or had firsthand experience of the extraordinary power of the fixer. In his book *Man Against Himself* (1938, 23), Karl Menninger (one of the leading experts on the effects of trauma on World War II troops) writes that suicide "is a murder of the self by the self." Suicide is the fixer's way of trying to fix the distressed mind-body by killing off the individual. It's the fixer at the height of its power.

1. Whenever your fixer is active during the day, notice your body tension, storylines, mental pressure, and behaviors. Note how the fixer creates mental pressure urging you to act. It can either drive your actions or leave you feeling overwhelmed and paralyzed. Be aware of the way your fixer frames the demand. The fixer traps you into thinking, *I need to, I have to, I must,* or *I should.* Do you recognize signs of your depressor when your fixer is in action? What do you notice?

   a.   Write your observations:

   _____

   _____

   _____

   _____

   _____

The real effect of the fixer is to keep the I-System going. In doing so, the fixer strengthens the damaged self. At times, the fixer uses positive thoughts like *Exercise more, Eat better, Sleep better, Work harder, Enjoy life,* or *Be a better parent,* hiding its underlying motive. However, when the fixer uses thoughts like *Pass everyone on the road, Punch out that son of a bitch, Snort more cocaine,* and *Get away from this turmoil,* its motives are clearer. Never underestimate the huge pressure the fixer creates when trying to fix the damaged self. You can't fight the fixer. For example, the urge to drink and take drugs may be from the fixer, but having another fixer that urges you to stop drinking and taking drugs just pours more fuel on the fire, creating a yo-yo effect. By actively becoming aware that the fixer is driving a particular activity, you decrease the fixer's power over you.

Chapter 4—Day Two cont.

b. Make a special note of any of your activities that have to do with addiction, risk taking, overworking, anger, and irritability. Do you recognize the mental and physical pressure the fixer exerts? Can you find the embedded depressor? Note the level of mental pressure with 0 for none, + for mild, ++ for moderate, or +++ for severe.

Situation or Action	Mental Pressure	Fixer	Depressor
Drinking too much	+++	I need a drink.	I'm a miserable wreck.
Working too hard	+++	I need to work harder.	I'll never get it done.
Being kept waiting	+++	Stomp out of the room.	I get no respect.

When active, does the fixer impair your judgment? Yes _____ No _____

Can you ever do enough to satisfy the fixer? Yes _____ No _____

Recognizing and befriending the embedded depressor is essential to reducing the excess mental and physical pressure the fixer causes. The fixer is powerless without the depressor.

Chapter 4—Day One cont.

2. Do a Fixer map. For several minutes, jot around the following oval any thoughts that come up about "How I Am Going to Improve My Life."

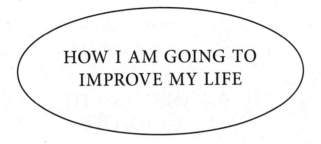

HOW I AM GOING TO
IMPROVE MY LIFE

a. For each thought on your map, write in the table below the type and location of any body tension and amount of mental pressure you feel when you think about trying to reach your goal.

b. For each thought, try to notice its embedded depressors and requirements.

Fixer Thought	Body Tension	Mental Pressure	Depressor	Requirement
Try harder to lose weight.	Chest and gut tight	++	I'm fat.	I should be slim.

It's important to recognize that your fixer items are generated by your fixer in response to your depressor to get you to meet your I-System requirements. When the I-System and its requirements are resting, so are the fixers or depressors. However, once an event or condition triggers the I-System by violating one of your requirements, the fixer, the depressor, and the storylines create the energy (commotion) that keeps the I-System going.

Chapter 4—Day Two cont.

3. Do the map again, this time using your bridging awareness practices. Before you start writing, listen to background sounds, feel your body's pressure on your seat, sense your feet on the floor, and feel the pen in your hand. Once you're settled, keep feeling the pen in your hand, and start writing. Scatter your thoughts around the oval. Watch the ink go onto the paper, and listen to background sounds.

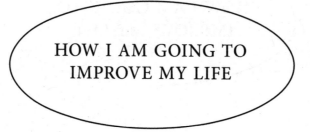

HOW I AM GOING TO
IMPROVE MY LIFE

a. How is this map the same as or different from the previous one?

_____

_____

b. Look at the thoughts on your map one at a time. Notice how much mental pressure and body tension you feel when you think about going for the goal in each of those thoughts. The thoughts that come with little body tension and mental pressure are from your natural functioning true self. For those thoughts with excess body tension, can you recognize the hidden requirement? List them:

_____

_____

Some thoughts on this map may look like thoughts on the previous Fixer map. On this map, mind-body bridging practices removed the excess mental and physical pressure that came with the fixer. As previously mentioned, when your awareness prevents the fixer from impairing your activities by creating excess mind clutter, body tension, and mental pressure, it's called befriending the fixer. This is when you are functioning naturally. The more you use your mind-body bridging practices in your daily life, the more you'll do things because you *want* to, rather than *have* to. Without the I-System's internal pressure (when your I-System is at rest), your daily activities will give you more pleasure and peace of mind. In this state, your PTSD heals.

Befriend Your Fixer

The only time you can recognize and befriend your fixer is in the moment during its activity when your I-System is on. This is when you can stop the cycle of the depressor and fixer and calm your I-System.

When your fixer is active, these steps will help:

1. During an activity, note any body tension, mental pressure, and spinning storylines that point to the fixer. (You may not have the slightest inkling that your mental or physical functioning is impaired.)

2. Use bridging awareness practices and thought labeling to quiet your I-System.

3. Remember that the I-System's depressor or fixer may spin new stories about why the fixer should keep going. These storylines impair your judgment and cause you to act in a way that makes you regretful afterward.

4. Recognize the underlying depressor and realize that the fixer's real motive is to repair the damaged self. (You already know the fixer can't fix the damaged self, because the fixer is part of the I-System.)

5. Remember, it's not the activity you are doing that matters as much as who's doing it, your true self or your damaged self.

Befriending the fixer is when your I-System is quiet, your body is calm, and your activities are being done by your true self and not the pressure-driven fixer. You witness, firsthand, that the damaged self is a false belief caused by your active I-System. You are not broken and don't need fixing.

DAY THREE   DATE: _____

Russ was doing well with his mind-body bridging practices, and shared with his group that he was sleeping better and had less tension and fewer PTSD symptoms. Every part of his life was changing, including his relationship with his wife. Then, with clenched hands, he angrily said, "Mind-body bridging isn't working anymore. I should have a job by now." His I-System had captured the thoughts *I can't let my family down* and *I should be more of a man*, and the body tension (pressure in his chest) that came with these thoughts meant his fixer was active. The depressor and fixer work together to keep the overactive I-System going. Everything he did to find a job increased his body tension. His mouth would go dry, making it hard to talk in job interviews, and his mind would clutter with thoughts like *Yes, I can do it* or *No, I can't.* After mapping his thoughts, Russ recognized his storyline: *If I were more of a man, getting a job would be as easy as calling friends and networking....* He recognized his requirement as *I should have a job by now*, and his depressor as *I'm not a man.* He realized his fixer had captured a thought that was from natural functioning, *I need to find a job*, adding pressure and extra tension to his misery. By recognizing and befriending his fixer in action (the only place you can recognize and befriend your fixer), Russ was able to stop the depressor and fixer's merry-go-round and find a job.

1. Throughout the day, notice and write how often your fixer is active. Look for depressor-fixer interplay, which creates storylines, body tension, and mental pressure.

    a. What happened?

    _____

    _____

    _____

    b. How did you befriend your fixer?

    _____

    _____

    _____

    c. What about your behaviors has changed or stayed the same?

    _____

    _____

    _____

Chapter 4—Day Three cont.

2. Do a To-Do map, by jotting down all the things you need to get done over the next few days. Write for three to four minutes. Note any body tension that comes with the activities. It may help to see the sample map that follows.

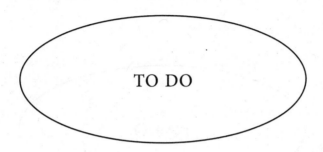

a. Try to tell the difference between the fixer and natural functioning. Remember, the naturally functioning true self comes out only when your I-System rests, which means there's no body tension.

Map Item	Body Tension	Fixer	Depressor	Natural Function?
Apply for VA benefits.	+++	Yes	I know they'll never give me what I need.	No
Pay electric bill.	Ø	No	None	Yes

b. Go back over your fixer items on your log, using your bridging awareness and thought labeling tools. What happens? Natural functioning is the engine of life. It's simply all the activities of your daily life without the I-System's adding anything or taking anything away.

Chapter 4—Day Three cont.

SAMPLE TO DO MAP

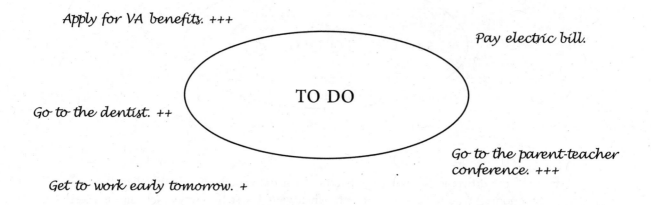

Prepare for tomorrow's meeting. ++

Apply for VA benefits. +++

Pay electric bill.

TO DO

Go to the dentist. ++

Go to the parent-teacher conference. +++

Get to work early tomorrow. +

Go for a run. +

Call Dad. +

DAY FOUR   DATE: _____

Remember Mary and her kids, from Day Two in this chapter? She had trouble telling the difference between thoughts the fixer produced and those from natural functioning until she remembered to use her bridging awareness practices. Now she comes out of the shower with a relatively calm mind and body. When she looks at the clock, thinks *The kids will be late for school*, and feels her shoulders tighten, she knows that her usual response of yelling, "You'll be late for school! Hurry up!" is a fixer. She listens to the traffic sounds outside the window, feels her feet as she walks across the hall, feels her shoulders drop, and calmly gathers everyone up. She befriends her fixer and returns to natural functioning.

Now that you can identify the activity of the fixer on your maps, it's time for you to befriend your fixer. Remember, the best time to befriend your fixer is right in the middle of an activity where you notice excess body tension, storylines, mental pressure, overwhelmed feelings, and so on. To befriend the fixer, you have to have a strong bridging awareness practice. Only when you know what it's like to have a quiet I-System can you recognize when your fixer is active, because the I-System is so disruptive that it's difficult to tell the difference between the fixer and natural functioning. The fixer is so persistent in our lives that most of us come to see its activity as "It's just me." How many times have you ignored your body tension and dismissed your mind clutter with an "it's just me" attitude? Remember, when your I-System is at rest, you can befriend your fixer by simply being aware of its activity and then bringing your awareness back to what you were doing.

1. During the day, notice the difference between activities prompted by your fixer and those that come from natural functioning.

Activity	Telltale Signs of Your Fixer	Mind-Body Bridging Practices Used	Results
Getting the kids ready for school	Breathing faster, toes curling, do-or-die sense of urgency	Listened to back-ground sounds, stayed aware of my body	Calmly got kids ready for school

Chapter 4—Day Four cont.

2. Do a map titled "What Will Happen to Me If I Give Up My Fixer." Jot whatever comes to mind when you imagine giving up your fixer (for example, *I won't have any motivation, I'll lose my job, I'll never accomplish anything, I won't be successful,* or *I'll never get well*). Write for three to four minutes. Describe your body tension at the bottom of the map.

$$\bigcirc$$

WHAT WILL
HAPPEN IF I GIVE UP
MY FIXER?

Body Tension:

_____

_____

a. Is your mind cluttered or clear?

_____

b. Is your body tense or relaxed?

_____

c. What are some of your requirements?

_____

d. In this mind-body state, how do you act?

_____

Some people feel panicked about this map. Their I-System is so strong that they feel that it's who they really are. They feel as if they'll lose who they are and have nothing left without their fixers. Some fears people have shared are: "To give up my fixer would be like giving up my right arm!" and "If I let my fixer go, I'll go right down the tubes."

Chapter 4—Day Four cont.

3. Do the previous map again, this time using your bridging awareness practices. Before you start writing, listen to background sounds, feel your body's pressure on your seat, sense your feet on the floor, and feel the pen in your hand. Once you're settled, keep feeling the pen in your hand, and start writing. Watch the ink go onto the paper, and listen to background sounds. Write for three to four minutes.

```
        WHAT WILL
   HAPPEN IF I GIVE UP
       MY FIXER?
```

a. How is this map the same or different from the previous one?

_____

_____

_____

_____

b. Can you experience your naturally functioning true self? Yes _____ No _____

With a quiet I-System, your true self functions naturally. In this unified, harmonious mind-body state, you access your power of healing, goodness, and wisdom to take care of yourself and your responsibilities.

DAY FIVE   DATE: _____

Larry's drinking was his attempt to fix his PTSD-ridden life. Throughout his day, he wove stories about why he craved alcohol. These storylines included his wife (*She talked to her sister all day and didn't clean the house and cook my supper....*) and even everyday driving (*I can't believe there are son many red lights. They don't know what they are doing....*). He also had stories about how he and his military unit were so close, how he could always depend on them, and how they were the only ones who understood him and what he was going through. The depressor and fixer's vicious cycle kept him living his life through his stories.

1. During the day, notice your storylines, driven by your depressor and fixer. Storylines draw heavily from past difficulties and future fears or wishes. Whether positive or negative, they keep you from being in the present. The way the depressor and fixer work together always creates a strong need and pressure to keep the story going. When you notice your I-System's storylines, your awareness shifts back to the task at hand. During an activity, can you shift from your I-System's storyline to natural functioning?

    a. Write the storylines you observed today, and notice any pressure from your depressor and fixer that kept the story going:

    _____

    _____

    _____

    _____

    b. What were your impulsive behaviors (drinking, overeating, anger, driving too fast, and so on) and the storylines you attached to them?

    _____

    _____

    _____

    c. When you became aware of your fixer, how were you able to befriend it and shift from your I-System's storyline to natural functioning?

    _____

    _____

    _____

    _____

Chapter 4—Day Five cont.

2. We all have something we want to do that, despite our intentions, we haven't done. In the oval, write the thing you find most difficult to do. Jot whatever comes to mind when you think about doing it. Write for three to four minutes. Describe your body tension at the bottom of the map.

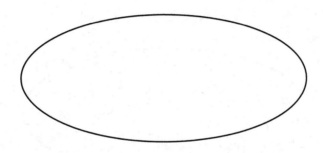

MY MOST DIFFICULT TO-DO

Body Tension:

_____

_____

a. Note the signs of your overactive I-System.

Body tension:	Yes ____ No ____	Mind clutter: Yes ____ No ____
Mental pressure:	Yes ____ No ____	Depressors: Yes ____ No ____
Fixers:	Yes ____ No ____	Storylines: Yes ____ No ____
Requirements:	Yes ____ No ____	

b. Do you see how your I-System is interfering with your life? Yes ____ No ____

3. Do the same map again, writing the same to-do in the next oval. Before you start writing, listen to background sounds, feel your body's pressure on your seat, sense your feet on the floor, and feel the pen in your hand. Once you're settled, keep feeling the pen in your hand, and start writing whatever comes to mind. Watch the ink go onto the paper, and listen to background sounds. Write for three to four minutes.

MY MOST DIFFICULT TO-DO WITH BRIDGING

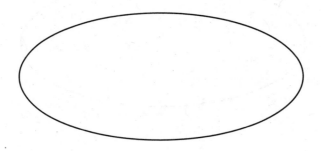

    a.   How is this map the same as or different from the previous one?

_____

_____

_____

    b.   Does your naturally functioning true self let you follow through with any needed action?
       Yes _____ No _____

DAY SIX   DATE: _____

Ted was irritable most of the time. Even the little things set him off. Prone to road rage, he often had to restrain himself from hurting others. For example, whenever someone drove too slowly, his neck bulged, face reddened, and head throbbed. Ted thought, *A guy driving twenty-five miles per hour in a forty-five-mile-per-hour zone should be shot!* He shared that he started using bridging awareness practices and thought labeling as effective tools to "cool myself down." Continuing his practices, he came to see that his multiple requirements—*The mail should be on time, I should not be put on hold, Others shouldn't speak disrespectfully about our country*—had created a physical meltdown that caused him to "hurt all over." As he came to realize that his anger was an attempt to fix himself and the world, his disposition changed. As a matter of fact, Ted shared that he and his wife were in the car, rushing to deal with a family emergency, when they came upon a car stopped at an intersection. Ted's wife told him to "get that guy moving." Ted got out of the car and, instead of getting angry, simply "saw an old guy who was lost, spent a few minutes calmly reassuring him by giving him directions, and then got back into the car." He then told us, "I had no idea I had that kindness in me."

1. Use all your mind-body bridging practices in your life today. Calm your mind and reduce your body tension with:

    ◆ Bridging awareness practices

    ◆ Thought labeling

    Now, with a calm mind and relaxed body, you can:

    ◆ Become aware of your storylines

    ◆ Recognize and release the depressor's activity (befriend your depressor)

    ◆ Recognize and release the fixer's activity (befriend your fixer)

    ◆ Recognize your requirements and release the I-System's activity (defuse your requirements)

    What mind-body bridging practices worked for you today?

    _____

    _____

    _____

    b. For what situations did they not work?

    _____

    _____

    _____

Chapter 4—Day Six cont.

2. Do a Situation map. From the previous step, choose the most distressing situation for which your mind-body bridging practices didn't work. Write the situation in the oval. Next, take a couple of minutes to scatter around the oval any thoughts that come to mind. Work quickly, without editing your thoughts. Describe your body tension at the bottom of the map.

SITUATION MAP

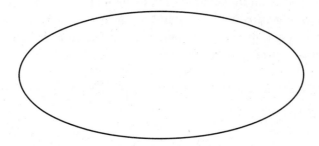

Body Tension:

_____

_____

    a. Is your mind cluttered or clear?

_____

    b. Is your body tense or relaxed?

_____

    c. List your depressors and fixers:

_____

_____

    d. List your requirements:

_____

_____

    e. In this mind-body state, how do you act?

_____

Chapter 4—Day Six cont.

3. Do the same map again, writing the same situation in the next oval. Before you start writing, listen to background sounds, feel your body's pressure on your seat, sense your feet on the floor, and feel the pen in your hand. Once you're settled, keep feeling the pen in your hand and start writing. Watch the ink go onto the paper and listen to background sounds. Write for a couple of minutes.

SITUATION MAP WITH BRIDGING

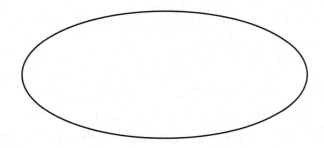

Observe the differences between the two maps:

a. Is your mind cluttered or clear?

_____

b. Is your body tense or relaxed?

_____

_____

c. In this mind-body state, how do you act?

_____

_____

_____

d. Are you better prepared now to deal with this situation? Yes _____ No _____

DAY SEVEN   DATE: _____

As situations come up in life, people often ask, "What should I do?" The real question is not *what* should you do, but *who* is doing it? If your I-System is overactive and your damaged self is in charge, then nothing you "should do" will ever be good enough. When your I-System rests, your true self is in the driver's seat. Your naturally functioning true self answers the question of what to do. The question is taken care of as your true self naturally takes the right action to solve the problem.

During the day, ask yourself who is doing the activity. (This can apply to any activity, be it walking, parenting, using the computer, paying bills, working, or playing.) Is it your true self arising from a quiet I-System, or your damaged self prompted by an overactive I-System? Notice how your life is changing with your mind-body bridging practices:

_____

_____

_____

_____

You are improving your life with your mind-body bridging practices. By recognizing and releasing the negative effects of your fixer, your progress and healing continue. The I-System is not a static system; it may try to fool you by creating more fixers. For your continued progress and healing, it's important to recognize these new fixers. Some examples are:

◆ *I'm doing better. I can relax and not do so much bridging.*

◆ *I'm calm now, so I can drink socially.*

◆ *I'm improved enough that I can do the maps in my head.*

◆ *It's okay to explode once in a while if the situation warrants it.*

◆ *I only need to bridge when I feel bad.*

◆ *If it feels good, I'm naturally functioning, and I should do it.*

◆ *Bridging means having free choice, so anytime I choose to go eighty miles per hour, it's okay.*

◆ *Natural functioning is always effortless, so I don't need to try anymore.*

The previous examples of fixers parade themselves as choices that come from natural functioning. But they come with the same distinctive signs you learned earlier in this chapter (body tension, mental pressure, urgent storylines, and lack of clarity about the effect of your actions). What *is* new about them is that they present themselves in a way that makes you feel good about them. This might cause you to fail to recognize them as fixers and instead see them as signs of progress. Only by befriending your fixer (see Day Four) can your true self make the choice, free of the I-System's influences.

MBB WEEKLY EVALUATION SCALE
WHY YOUR BEST EFFORTS SEEM TO GO WRONG

Date: _____

During the past week, how was it for you to do these practices? Check the description that best matches your practice: hardly ever, occasionally, usually, or almost always.

How often do you...	Hardly Ever	Occasionally	Usually	Almost Always
Notice the fixer's drive, tension, and never-ending nature?				
Become aware of the body sensations that came with the fixer?				
Recognize the fixer's defeating nature?				
Realize that the fixer can never fix the damaged self?				
Find the depressor embedded in the fixer?				
See the interplay of the fixer and the depressor?				
Recognize the storylines that came with the fixer?				
Notice the difference between activities the fixer produced and those from natural functioning?				
Notice the release of tension and excess drive when you befriended your fixer through awareness?				
Function better at home and at work?				

List the main body sensations you have when the fixer is in control:

_____

List three behaviors the fixer causes:

_____

_____

List three themes of storylines that come with the fixer:

_____

_____

How did your behavior change when you befriended your fixer and functioned naturally?

_____

MBB QUALITY OF LIFE SCALE

Date: _____

It's time to do another MBB Quality of Life Scale to see your progress. Fill out this quality of life scale, and compare it with the one you did in chapter 1, Day One. Congratulate yourself on your improved scores. Note any areas of low scores. Low scores relate to requirements you haven't yet become aware of or defused. The rest of this workbook gives more skills to help you deal with the underlying requirements that still negatively affect your life. This workbook records your journey of self-discovery and self-healing.

Over the past seven days, how did you do in these areas?

Circle the number under your answer.	Not at all	Several days	More than half the days	Nearly every day
1. I've been interested in doing things.	0	1	3	5
2. I've felt optimistic, excited, and hopeful.	0	1	3	5
3. I've slept well and woken up feeling rested.	0	1	3	5
4. I've had lots of energy.	0	1	3	5
5. I've been able to focus on tasks and use self-discipline.	0	1	3	5
6. I've stayed healthy, eaten well, exercised, and had fun.	0	1	3	5
7. I've felt good about my relationships with my family and friends.	0	1	3	5
8. I've been satisfied with my accomplishments at home, work, or school.	0	1	3	5
9. I'm comfortable with my financial situation.	0	1	3	5
10. I feel good about the spiritual base of my life.	0	1	3	5
11. I'm satisfied with the direction of my life.	0	1	3	5
12. I'm fulfilled, with a sense of well-being and peace of mind.	0	1	3	5
Column Totals:	___	___	___	___

Total Score: _____

WORK TOWARD RESOLVING YOUR PTSD

Over the past month, you have learned mind-body bridging foundation tools and have started healing your PTSD. The rest of this workbook specifically focuses on the PTSD symptoms that interfere with your quality of life.

The diagram in figure 5.1 shows what can happen to your thoughts. In the upper I-System loop, the thought becomes a requirement that switches on the depressor-fixer cycle. This impairs how your mind and body work, which in turn causes you to feel and act damaged (dysfunctional mind-body).

In the lower *natural loop*, your thoughts and actions are free from the I-System. In this unified state, you experience harmony and balance, and live your life at its best. No matter who you are or what you've been through, right here, right now, you can experience and express your true self. Your true self is always present. It doesn't depend on an idealized image or the ability to mimic good behavior. The natural loop isn't something to aim for; it's always with you, and you experience it automatically when your I-System rests. This is where you heal your PTSD.

The *I-System loop* keeps your PTSD symptoms going. In this loop, your mind clutter, body tension, and restricted awareness affect how you think, feel, see the world, and act, impairing your ability to heal yourself. It isn't your traumatic experience that puts you in the I-System loop; it's your requirements related to the trauma that activate your I-System.

In this chapter, you will map any requirements you have for yourself, others, and situations. The more you are in the natural functioning loop, the quicker and easier it'll be to recognize and defuse your requirements. *Defusing a requirement* simply means recognizing it, having that "aha" moment, and being able to let go of that requirement. This happens only in real time—during the situation or activity. Consistently using your mind-body bridging practices means you'll live more and more of your life in the self-healing natural loop.

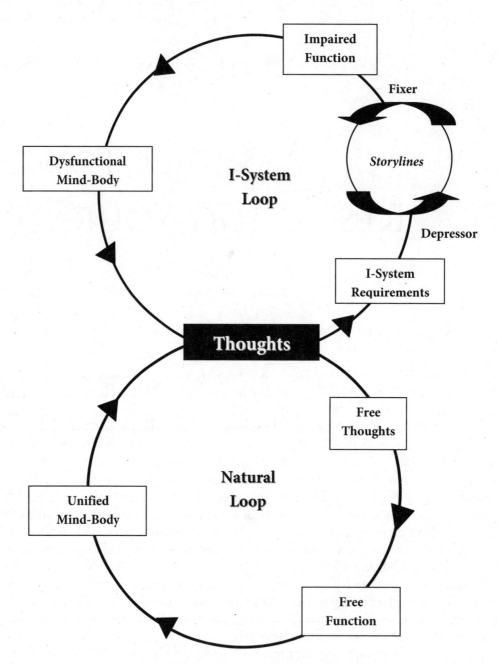

Figure 5.1   The I-System Loop and the Natural Loop

The natural loop is your birthright, is always present, and is where you experience your true self. This is where healing yourself takes place. Your requirements for yourself and the world pull you up into the I-System loop, where the mind-body commotion of the I-System impairs your life and keeps your PTSD symptoms going.

DAY ONE   DATE: _____

John works at a local auto parts store. On his second day at work, a coworker asks him how many people he killed in Iraq. John begins to think, *Who the hell does this guy think he is, asking me that question? He should know you don't ask a combat veteran how many people he's killed.* John's teeth clench and his body starts filling with tension as his mind starts replaying war events. John's I-System has been activated by his requirement *No one should ask me questions about Iraq.* As he shakes his head and walks away from his coworker, his tension builds. He mulls over his storylines: *No one should approach me like that. I served my country honorably. This guy has no idea what Iraq was like and how hard it's been since I got home.* Once activated by a requirement, the depressor-fixer cycle works to keep the I-System going. The depressor takes any thoughts of Iraq that come to mind, spins a storyline, and creates a painful mind-body state. The fixer jumps in and tries to relieve that painful emotional state with tension-driven, impulsive actions. By the time John reaches the stockroom, the signs and symptoms of an acute state of mind-body distress are clear. His thoughts are angry and swirling, his thinking completely self-directed, his body full of tension, and his face tight and frowning. John then seeks out the insensitive employee, and as he nears the person, his vision narrows, his eyes glare, and his thoughts become less clear. John then grabs the employee's arm and yells, "Don't ever ask me that question again." He stares intently and angrily into this man's eyes before releasing his arm and storming away. This aggressive act is the fixer's way of trying to repair the agitated mind-body state the depressor caused.

1. Observe yourself during the day whenever you become upset, tense, irritable, or overwhelmed, or have a flare-up of your PTSD symptoms.

Situation	Requirement	What Happened
Erik's stupid remark upset me.	*Erik shouldn't make stupid remarks.*	*Didn't recognize requirement and was upset all day.*

2. Map the most disturbing experience you had today that another person's behavior caused. Write the behavior at the top of the map (for example, *My boss lied to me*), and write how you wanted that person to act (for example, *My boss shouldn't lie*) in the center of the oval. Take four to five minutes to scatter your thoughts around the oval as you think about that person's behavior. Describe your body tension at the bottom of the map.

DISTURBING EXPERIENCE MAP

Other Person's Behavior: _____

Body Tension:

_____

_____

   a. Is your body tense? Yes _____ No _____

   b. Is your mind cluttered? Yes _____ No _____

   c. Is your distress due to the other person's behavior? Yes _____ No _____

   d. Is the distress due to the requirement in the oval? Yes _____ No _____

   If you believe the distress was from the other person's behavior, you are letting yourself be victimized by circumstances. As long as you do *not* recognize that how you wanted the other person to act is *your* requirement, you will suffer distress and stay in the I-System loop. Simply recognizing your requirement and seeing what that requirement is doing to you prompts a dramatic mental and physical shift so that you are no longer a victim of circumstance.

Chapter 5—Day One cont.

3. Experience for yourself whether or not you are a victim of circumstance. Write the same behavior on the following line, and in the oval, write how you wanted the other person to be. Before you continue writing, listen to background sounds, feel your body's pressure on your seat, sense your feet on the floor, and feel the pen in your hand. Once you're settled, keep feeling the pen in your hand and start writing. Watch the ink go onto the paper and listen to background sounds.

DISTURBING EXPERIENCE MAP WITH BRIDGING

Other Person's Behavior: _____

a. How is this map the same as or different from the previous one?

_____

_____

_____

b. Are you a victim of circumstance? Yes _____ No _____

Do you see how, on the previous map, the statement in the oval was a requirement because it activated your I-System? On this map, the same statement in the oval is *not* a requirement. It's a natural thought, because your I-System was calm, and your body tension and mental clutter reduced dramatically. You are now prepared to deal with that situation with a clear mind and relaxed body. Your mind-body bridging practice doesn't take away your natural expectations of how others should behave, but it does take away the devastation your requirements cause, which prepares you to heal yourself and deal actively and confidently with your life circumstances.

DAY TWO   DATE: _____

Rita, who was brutally raped four years ago, felt anxious about having flashbacks, because she always felt overwhelmed whenever she had one. She began attending a women's group that used the principles in this workbook. Using mind-body bridging tools, she recognized her requirement: *I shouldn't have flashbacks.* She then asked, "How will my knowing my requirement stop my flashbacks?" The group leader explained that a flashback is a reliving of the unhealed wound the traumatic events caused. The more Rita worked on calming her I-System, the more chances she had to heal herself. A couple of weeks later, she reported having fewer flashbacks, and more important, she said that when they did occur, they were "less earth-shaking, and I no longer experienced myself as soiled, dirty, and spoiled." Using her mind-body bridging practices, she experienced a new, expansive self and said, "I'm bigger than my flashbacks."

1. Log any situations that prompt you to become upset, tense, irritable, anxious, or overwhelmed or that bring on your PTSD symptoms. Realize that always underlying the situation is a requirement you weren't aware of, not the event that's "causing" your distress. Recognizing the requirement prompts changes in your thoughts, actions, and PTSD symptoms.

Situation	How You Handled the Situation	Unfulfilled Requirements
My spouse said I'll never change.	I yelled, "Go to hell!" and didn't talk to him all day.	My spouse should accept me.
I couldn't find my car keys.	I exhausted myself looking for them and became depressed.	I should know where I put my car keys.

Chapter 5—Day Two cont.

2. Do a Today My Crisis Is… map. Pick a situation from the previous log that was a crisis and write it in the oval. Take three to four minutes to jot whatever thoughts come to mind. Describe your body tension at the bottom of the map.

```
        TODAY MY CRISIS
             IS…
    _____
    _____
```

Body Tension:

_____

_____

Were your PTSD symptoms increased in the crisis? Yes _____ No _____

Identify the requirements on your map (for example, if today's crisis for you is *I don't have enough money to pay my bills*, a requirement would be *I should have enough money to pay the bills*).

_____

_____

_____

_____

_____

Your I-System's commotion machine has you feeling distressed, bitter, angry, and hopeless, and believing that anyone in your shoes would feel the same way. Now ask yourself, *Isn't it bad enough that our economy is in the tank? Why do I have to let my I-System cause a personal meltdown, limiting my natural ability to solve my money problems?* You have no control over the current financial crisis or others' behavior. You *do* have control over defusing *your* requirements and healing your PTSD.

Chapter 5—Day Two cont.

3. Do another map on the same crisis, this time using your bridging awareness practices. Write the crisis in the next oval. Before you continue writing, listen to background sounds, feel your body's pressure on your seat, sense your feet on the floor, and feel the pen in your hand. Once you are settled, keep feeling the pen in your hand, as you write your thoughts for the next few minutes. Watch the ink go onto the paper and listen to background sounds.

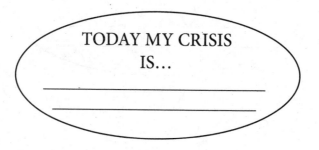

a. How did your mind-body state differ between the two maps?

_____

_____

b. Which mind-body state lets you handle the crisis better?

_____

c. Can you see that it's your I-System, not the event, that's causing your distress?

_____

_____

You now know firsthand that it's your I-System, not the event, causing your misery and preventing you from healing yourself. Also, this activity shows the power of building a strong daily bridging awareness practice. When you feel body tension, use your bridging awareness tools to create the emotional space to defuse requirements during your busy day.

Steps to Recognize and Defuse Requirements

Having a flare-up of your PTSD symptoms or becoming distressed and overwhelmed means you have a hidden requirement you aren't yet aware of. Use these steps to help you recognize and defuse your requirements:

1. Begin developing your skills by using them in simple situations—like when waiting for a long red light, experiencing a dropped phone call, or dealing with impolite clerks—and gradually build to using the skills in more complex relationships and situations.

2. Become aware of the earliest signs of an overactive I-System (such as noticing specific body tension, as well as depressor, fixer, and storyline activity), and let them prompt you to look for the underlying requirement.

3. Use your bridging awareness practice and thought labeling tools to interrupt the I-System's commotion machine and clearly identify the underlying requirement. Realize that it's *your* requirement about the activity, person, or situation—*not* the activity, person, or situation—that's causing your distress.

4. Once you feel a release (gradually or suddenly) about the situation, you have defused your requirement. That previously out-of-control devastation melts into a more manageable disappointment. Describe what happened when you used your mind-body bridging tools to defuse your requirements in a meltdown situation. Here's an example of what a client wrote:

> Recently, I learned that my twelve-year-old son was smoking. I became enraged, screaming at him and threatening him, which gave me a migraine. Later, when I learned he was smoking again, I felt my jaw tighten. Noticing this signal, I realized my I-System was switched on. I then listened to the sound of the dogs barking outside, which made me feel more settled and helped me see my requirement: *My twelve-year-old son shouldn't smoke.* I was now clear that it was *my* requirement, not just his behavior, that caused my added distress. I was really disappointed in my son, but didn't melt down. I was able to calm myself down enough to discuss the situation with my son, and felt we were gaining on the problem.

_____

_____

_____

_____

Now, in the larger vessel of your expansive true self (review figure 1.1), your body settles, your thinking clears, and your choices flow. You're healing your PTSD symptoms.

DAY THREE   DATE: _____

1. Throughout the day, focus on your relationships. Notice any signs of an overactive I-System: body tension, cluttered mind, storylines, and depressor-fixer activity. What did the other person do that activated your I-System? How did you react? Did you recognize the hidden requirements?

    a. Observe the signs of an overactive I-System in your relationships:

Other Person's Behavior	Your Reaction or Behavior	Your Requirements
Kim wouldn't talk to me. She was cold.	Felt heavy pressure in my chest, lots of negative self-talk, stomped out of the house	Kim should talk to me when I want; Kim shouldn't be cold.

    b. Now that you can see it was your requirement, not the other person's behavior, that caused your distress, are you ready to defuse your requirements in real time, as you go about your life? Yes _____ No _____

    Defusing requirements and healing yourself go hand in hand.

Chapter 5—Day Three cont.

2. Do a Requirement map. From the log you just did, choose someone whose behavior brought on your PTSD symptoms or caused you the most distress. Write that person's name in the oval. Around the oval, scatter your requirements for how you want that person to act; label these "R". Next, under each requirement, write what thoughts ("T") you have when the other person does *not* meet that requirement. Below each thought, note whatever body tension ("BT") you have when the other person doesn't meet your requirement. Take your time doing this map. See the sample map that follows.

REQUIREMENT MAP

MY RELATIONSHIP
REQUIREMENTS FOR:

_____

a. In this mind-body state, how do you act?

_____

b. Are you starting to see how your requirements affect your relationship?
Yes _____ No _____

c. Do you think the distress just shown is interfering with your ability to heal yourself from PTSD? Yes _____ No _____

d. Use your bridging awareness practices and thought labeling, and go back over your relationship requirements. What happens?

_____

_____

_____

Chapter 5—Day Three cont.

SAMPLE REQUIREMENT MAP

(R)   *He needs to do more around the house.*
(T)   *I do all the work, and I feel angry and taken for granted.*
(BT)   *Tight chest*

(R)   *He should take me out once a week.*
(T)   *I feel frustrated and ignored.*
(BT)   *Headache*

(R)   *She should respect how hard I work.*
(T)   *I don't get any slack; I should be able to relax.*
(BT)   *Shoulders tight*

MY RELATIONSHIP REQUIREMENTS FOR:
_____

(R)   *He should appreciate me.*
(T)   *Why doesn't he appreciate me?*
(BT)   *Stomachache*

(R)   *He should compliment me more.*
(T)   *I feel he doesn't care.*
(BT)   *Tight chest*

(R)   *She should pay attention to me when I'm present.*
(T)   *I feel angry and unimportant.*
(BT)   *Sinking feeling in stomach*

(R) = Requirement
(T) = Unfulfilled requirement thoughts
(BT) = Body tension

Chapter 5—Day Three cont.

3. Write the name of the person from the previous map in the next oval. Next, choose the requirement that still causes you the most distress when it's not met (for example, *He should respect me*) and write that on the line. Now scatter your thoughts around the oval, describing how things would look if that person *did* meet that requirement. Use as much detail as possible. For example, if the requirement choice is *He should respect me*, you might write, *He should not raise his voice, He should always call me when he's running late, He should talk to me before making a big decision,* or *He should be nice to my family.*

Requirement I Most Want Met: _____

HOW WOULD
THINGS LOOK IF
_____
MET MY REQUIREMENT?

a. Do you really think this will happen? Yes _____ No _____

b. Does this map show how useless it is to try to meet your requirements? Yes _____ No _____

c. Can you see that it's your requirement for how the other person should act that's causing your distress? Yes _____ No _____

d. Using your bridging awareness practices and thought labeling, go back over your requirement. What happens?

_____

_____

   The release in body tension shows that when the situation comes up again, you are prepared to defuse your requirements.

e. Can you see how this would change your relationship and let you heal yourself? Yes _____ No _____

DAY FOUR   DATE: _____

1. Throughout the day, focus on your troubling relationships. Notice any signs of an overactive I-System (such as body tension, cluttered mind, storylines, or depressor-fixer activity).

   a. When you saw the signs of your overactive I-System, what was the other person's behavior that activated your I-System? *Example: Kim was cold to me.*

   _____

   _____

   b. How did you react? What was your behavior? *Example: Felt pressure building in my chest and saw my negative self-talk; felt my feet on the ground and calmed down. I even felt okay about staying in the same room with her.*

   _____

   _____

   c. What storylines did you recognize? *Example: She doesn't love me...*

   _____

   _____

   d. List the requirements you recognized. *Example: Kim should always show me affection.*

   _____

   _____

   _____

   e. When you were faced today with a situation that used to set off your I-System, did you defuse some requirements? List them. *Example: Before, whenever Kim was cold, I felt totally bad, got mad, and stomped out of the house. Now, I realize it was my requirement that made me feel miserable. So I stayed home, and we watched TV.*

   _____

   _____

   _____

Chapter 5—Day Four cont.

2. Do a Requirement map. In the oval, write the name of the person who continues to trouble you the most. Around the oval, scatter your requirements for how that person should act. Next, under each requirement, write any body tension you have when the other person does *not* meet your requirement.

MY REQUIREMENTS
FOR:

_____

a. Is your mind cluttered or clear?

_____

b. Is your body tense or relaxed?

_____

_____

c. In this mind-body state, how do you act?

_____

_____

_____

_____

Your requirements for how people should act keep your PTSD going, which prevents you from healing.

3. Do another Requirement map, this time using your bridging awareness practices. Write the same person's name in the oval. Before you continue writing, listen to background sounds, feel your body's pressure on your seat, sense your feet on the floor, and feel the pen in your hand. Once you're settled, keep feeling the pen in your hand and start writing any thoughts that come to mind about how that person should act. Watch the ink go onto the paper and keep listening to background sounds.

⬭ **MY REQUIREMENTS FOR:** _____

Observe the differences between the two maps:

a. How do your thoughts on this map about how that person should act differ from those on the previous map?

_____

b. Now, what body sensations do you notice when you imagine that person failing to do what you put on this map?

_____

The absence of body tension means the thought is not a requirement.

c. In the mind-body state you noted previously, how do you act?

_____

_____

d. Are you now ready to defuse, in real time, the requirements you listed on your previous map? Yes _____ No _____

This exercise lets you know firsthand that it's your I-System, not the other person's behavior, that causes your distress.

DAY FIVE   DATE: _____

The simple act of recognizing a requirement starts changing your thoughts and actions, and makes healing possible. Today's exercise is about recognizing and defusing additional requirements you have for other people and for situations. For the more difficult-to-defuse requirements, it helps to first focus on small bits of behaviors and situations; for example, rather than deal with a general behavior like *My boss doesn't appreciate me*, break it down into many smaller, specific behaviors: *the way he looks at me, the way he smiles at others, the critical tone of his voice, the sharp words he uses.* This allows you to recognize very specific requirements: *He should look at me kindly, he should smile at me, he should speak in a supportive voice,* and *he should use gentle words.* Next, use your bridging awareness practices on each of these separate requirements. Remember, after you recognize a requirement, it's ready to be defused.

1. What did you notice today?

_____

_____

_____

_____

_____

_____

_____

_____

_____

_____

_____

_____

_____

Can you now face that same situation without getting too distressed and with natural functioning? At stake here are not only your relationships but also your ability to heal yourself from PTSD.

Chapter 5—Day Five cont.

2. The purpose of mapping is to see your I-System in action. Let your I-System "run wild" on the next map. This is a great way to recognize your requirements. Do a map about a situation that upset you today. Write that situation in the oval and scatter your thoughts around it for the next few minutes. Describe your body tension at the bottom of the map.

SITUATION MAP

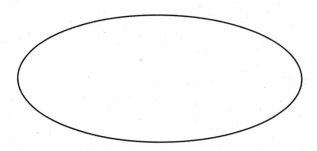

Body Tension:

_____

_____

a. Is your mind cluttered or clear?

_____

b. Is your body tense or relaxed?

_____

c. Identify your requirements:

_____

d. In this mind-body state, how do you act?

_____

Chapter 5—Day Five cont.

3. Do another map, writing the same situation in the next oval. Before you continue writing, listen to background sounds, feel your body's pressure on your seat, sense your feet on the floor, and feel the pen in your hand. Once you're settled, keep feeling the pen in your hand and start writing thoughts that come to mind. Watch the ink go onto the paper and listen to background sounds.

SITUATION MAP WITH BRIDGING

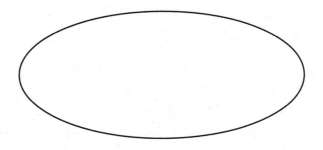

    a. Is your mind cluttered or clear?

_____

_____

    b. Is your body tense or relaxed?

_____

_____

    c. Notice the difference between the two maps:

        i. Do you now know firsthand that it's your I-System, not the event, that's causing your distress? Yes _____ No _____

       ii. Do you feel confident in your mind-body bridging skills? Yes _____ No _____
           If not, go back and review the tools you practiced on Day Two of this chapter.

DAY SIX   DATE: _____

Today, recognize and defuse your requirements as they come up.

1. Describe which mind-body bridging practices worked and which didn't.

_____

_____

_____

_____

_____

_____

_____

_____

2. List the requirements you were able to defuse today and those you were *not* able to successfully defuse.

Was Able to Defuse	Could Not Defuse

Chapter 5—Day Six cont.

3. Do a How My World Would Look If My Requirements Were Met map. Be as specific as possible; for example, *My spouse would always take care of me, Jason would not be an ass, My neighbor would mind his own business, My coworkers would do their jobs.* It may be helpful to refer to the "Could Not Defuse" list you just made.

HOW MY WORLD WOULD LOOK IF MY REQUIREMENTS WERE MET

Observations:

_____

_____

_____

_____

_____

_____

_____

_____

Even if your spouse, boss, friend, or neighbor met all your requirements, you would always have more left unfulfilled because your I-System always says, *Enough is never enough.* Defusing requirements is a skill that will help you throughout your life.

DAY SEVEN   DATE: _____

1. Do a map about a situation that upset you today. Write the situation in the oval, and scatter your thoughts about it around the oval. Describe your body tension at the bottom of the map.

SITUATION MAP

Body Tension:

_____

_____

   a. How did you handle that situation?

_____

_____

   b. What are your requirements?

_____

_____

     Slowly go over the items on your map and your requirements while using your favorite bridging awareness practice and thought labeling. Notice what happens. Are you now in a better position to defuse your requirements and face a similar situation in the future without getting distressed? Yes _____ No _____

Chapter 5—Day Seven cont.

2. Do a What Will Happen If I Let Go of All My Requirements for Others map. Scatter your thoughts around the next oval for several minutes.

$$\text{WHAT WILL HAPPEN IF I LET GO OF ALL MY REQUIREMENTS FOR OTHERS}$$

a. Does your I-System's commotion machine leave you feeling weak and fearful, and believing you will lose control of your life? Yes _____ No _____

b. Write your level of body tension by each item, using Ø for none, + for minimal, ++ for moderate, or +++ for severe. See the sample map that follows. Next list any items that come with body tension and their underlying requirements:

Item with Body Tension	Requirement

SAMPLE NO REQUIREMENT MAP

I'm unprotected. +++

Bill will take advantage of me. +++

Nothing will be done right. +++

WHAT WILL HAPPEN IF I LET GO OF ALL MY REQUIREMENTS FOR OTHERS

Mary will see me as weak. +++

I'll have more time. Ø

Item with Body Tension	Requirement
I'm unprotected. +++	*I should have protection.*
Nothing will be done right. +++	*I should do things right.*
Bill will take advantage of me. +++	*Bill shouldn't take advantage of me.*
Mary will see me as weak. +++	*Mary shouldn't see me as weak.*

Chapter 5—Day Seven cont.

3. Do the map again, this time using your bridging awareness practices. Before you start writing, listen to background sounds, feel your body's pressure on your seat, sense your feet on the floor, and feel the pen in your hand. Once you're settled, keep feeling the pen in your hand, and start writing your thoughts. Watch the ink go onto the paper, and listen to background sounds.

WHAT WILL
HAPPEN IF I LET GO OF ALL
MY REQUIREMENTS
FOR OTHERS

What are the differences between the two maps?

_____

_____

_____

_____

_____

_____

Is it becoming clearer that having requirements is destructive to you and your world? Requirements paralyze your ability to heal your PTSD and deal effectively with other people and situations. When you befriend your I-System, your true self can respond actively, attentively, and assertively in your relationships and situations. You'll be able to face each moment while having full access to your own wellspring of healing, goodness, and wisdom.

MBB WEEKLY EVALUATION SCALE
WORK TOWARD RESOLVING YOUR PTSD

Date: _____

During the past week, how did you do with these practices? Check the description that best matches your practice: hardly ever, occasionally, usually, or almost always.

How often do you...	Hardly Ever	Occasionally	Usually	Almost Always
Realize that having requirements always triggers your I-System and impairs your healing and functioning?				
Realize that requirements you aren't aware of cause your daily upsets?				
Keep from getting upset by defusing a requirement?				
See that your requirements trap you and keep your PTSD going?				
Notice a reduction in your PTSD symptoms?				
Experience the damaged self as a myth of the I-System?				
Recognize natural functioning?				
Realize that all you need to do to act from your true self is quiet your I-System so that natural functioning follows?				
Appreciate your true self as coming moment by moment from natural functioning?				
Experience that you are connected to a wellspring of healing, goodness, and wisdom?				
Appreciate parts of everyday life in a new light?				
Notice that your relationships have improved?				
Function better at home and at work?				
Handle crisis situations better?				

List three requirements that used to cause you to have a meltdown but that you now defuse by releasing the I-System's tension and letting yourself function naturally:

_____

_____

_____

CHAPTER 6

HEAL THE NEGATIVE
SELF-BELIEFS THAT
TRAUMA CAUSES

After a traumatic experience, natural thoughts like *I could have done more*, *I'll never be the same*, and *Why me?* come up. By latching on to negative self-talk, the I-System creates repetitive storylines that embed negativity into your body, over time leading to mental and physical distress. You develop a self-belief that because of the trauma or the way you acted during the crisis, you are damaged.

A *negative self-belief* is a dysfunctional mind-body state filled with negative thoughts about your traumatic experience. The only reason the negative self-beliefs continue is that you still have requirements for yourself. Negative self-beliefs can't last very long when your I-System is resting and your true self is running the show.

In the last chapter, you found that you get distressed from having unfulfilled requirements for the world. This chapter focuses on the requirements you have for yourself and on healing the negative self-beliefs trauma causes.

The requirements you have for yourself are keeping you from being who you really are and healing your PTSD. There's a difference between meeting your requirements and defusing requirements, as you'll see in the next exercise. When you defuse negative self-belief requirements, they lose their power over you and healing happens.

DAY ONE   DATE: _____

Today, notice situations in which you get distressed because of your requirements for yourself (for example, *I should know the answer when my boss asks me a question, I should please my spouse, I shouldn't be alone, I shouldn't make a mistake*).

1. List three situations in which your requirements for yourself activated your I-System today.

Situation	Requirement for Yourself	Depressor-Fixer Activity
At our morning meeting, my boss asked me a question.	I should know the answer when my boss asks me a question.	Depressor: I'm too stupid to know. Fixer: I'll be better prepared next time.

Fill out this chart based on what you listed in the last one:

Body tension and its location when your requirement *is* met	Body tension and its location when your requirement is *not* met
Example: I know the answer. Throat tight, stomach tight, sweaty hands, foot jiggles	Example: I don't know the answer. Face hot, pressure in my chest, throat closing, have to go to the bathroom

Chapter 6—Day One cont.

2. Fill out the next chart for each requirement from the previous step:

Storylines when meeting requirement	Storylines when not meeting requirement
It's a relief, It's over, There's always another meeting tomorrow	I'll never have everything they want, It's my fault because I'm not good enough, It's always the same

The I-System has you between a rock and a hard place. When your requirements for yourself aren't met, your depressor moves into the driver's seat, leaving you feeling damaged. Even when you are able to meet your requirements, the fixer moves into the driver's seat and enough is never enough. But when you defuse your requirement and your true self is in the driver's seat, you are naturally healing your negative self-belief, and you will take the right action moment by moment.

Do you see that it's not a matter of meeting or not meeting requirements, but defusing them? Yes _____ No _____

3. Using your bridging awareness practices, listen to background sounds, feel your body's pressure on your seat, sense your feet on the floor, and feel the pen in your hand. When you're settled, label your thoughts and go over each requirement you listed in today's first chart.

    What have you noticed about each of your requirements after mind-body bridging?

    Requirement One:

    _____

    _____

    Requirement Two:

    _____

    _____

    Requirement Three:

    _____

    _____

Tools to Defuse Requirements for Yourself

To defuse these requirements for yourself, use these tools:

1. Become aware of your earliest signs of an overactive I-System (body tension and depressor, fixer, and storyline activity), which will prompt you to look for the hidden requirement.

2. Use your bridging awareness practice and thought labeling tools to interrupt the I-System's commotion.

3. Recognize that it's *your* requirement for yourself, *not* the situation, causing your distress. For example, failing a test isn't what's distressing you; you're distressed because you have the requirement *I should have passed the test.*

4. You'll know you have defused the requirement when you feel a release of body tension and mind clutter. When the situation comes up again, your true self is in the driver's seat and you are able to deal with it calmly.

_____

_____

_____

DAY TWO   DATE: _____

1. Whenever you fail to meet your requirements, the I-System makes you feel like a failure. This reinforces your negative self-beliefs. Today's exercise focuses on requirements you have for yourself in your relationships with coworkers, in-laws, neighbors, grocery clerks, and so on (for example, *I shouldn't be so angry with my mother-in-law, I should give my coworkers timely feedback, I should be more caring*).

   a. What requirements do you have for yourself in your relationships? *Example: I should be more caring toward Mari.*

   _____

   _____

   b. What effect does each of these requirements have on you? *Example: I have to force myself to be caring, and deep down I feel like I am a bad husband.*

   _____

   _____

   _____

   c. How do these requirements affect your relationships? *Example: It spoils the relationship; I go from trying to care to not caring at all.*

   _____

   _____

2. List your requirements for yourself in your most important relationships, being as specific and detailed as possible (for example, *I shouldn't criticize Jay when he's late, I shouldn't upset T. J. when he's tired, I should make Sherri happy*). Do your requirements improve or limit the relationship?

Requirements	Improve	Limit

   Once you have a requirement (for example, *I shouldn't be critical or angry*), do you feel pressured or driven to meet that requirement? Do you feel bad about yourself if you don't meet it?

   _____

   _____

Chapter 6—Day Two cont.

3. Map your requirements for yourself in your most important relationship. Write the person's name in the oval. Around the oval, scatter your thoughts about how you should be in that relationship. There's no right or wrong. Be specific and work quickly.

> ## HOW I SHOULD BE IN MY MOST IMPORTANT
> ## RELATIONSHIP MAP

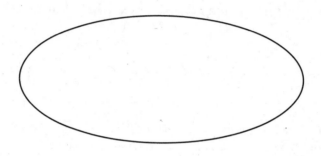

a. Look at each thought and notice any body tension you have when you think about meeting that requirement for how to be in that relationship. Look again at each item and notice your body tension when you are *not* meeting that requirement. Thoughts that come with body tension are your requirements.

b. Your requirements keep your negative self-beliefs going. What are your requirements?

_____

_____

_____

_____

_____

Chapter 6—Day Two cont.

4. Do the map again, writing the person's name in the oval. Before you continue writing, listen to background sounds, feel your body's pressure on your seat, sense your feet on the floor, and feel the pen in your hand. Once you're settled, keep feeling the pen in your hand, and start writing any thoughts that come to mind about that relationship. As you write, keep paying attention to background sounds, feeling the pen in your hand, and watching the ink go onto the paper. Write for three to four minutes.

HOW I SHOULD BE IN MY MOST IMPORTANT RELATIONSHIP WITH BRIDGING MAP

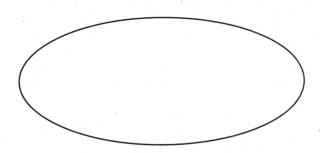

The release of body tension means you have moved from the I-System loop into the natural loop (see figure 5.1), where you can now function naturally. Although you still have thoughts about how you should be in your relationship, this release of body tension frees you to carry on in the relationship in a totally different way.

a. In this mind-body state, how do you act?

_____

_____

b. How can this map help you in your relationship?

_____

_____

When your overactive I-System switches off, you let go of your requirements about your most important relationship and create new opportunities.

Chapter 6—Day Two cont.

5. Do a How I Want to Be map. *Inside* the circle, write how you would like to be right here, right now (for example, *organized, healthy, strong, calm, brave*). Be specific! After you have listed at least six qualities, write the opposite of each quality *outside* the circle. Connect the quality inside the circle with a line to its opposite outside the circle. If needed, see the sample map that follows.

I WANT TO BE RIGHT HERE, RIGHT NOW MAP

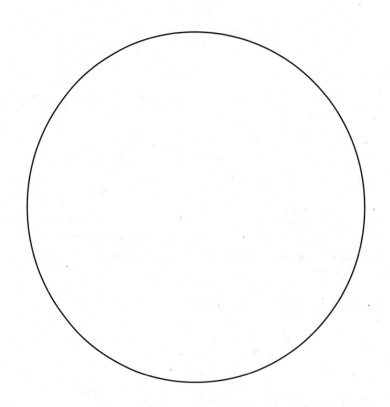

Chapter 6—Day Two cont.

SAMPLE MAP: I WANT TO BE RIGHT HERE, RIGHT NOW MAP

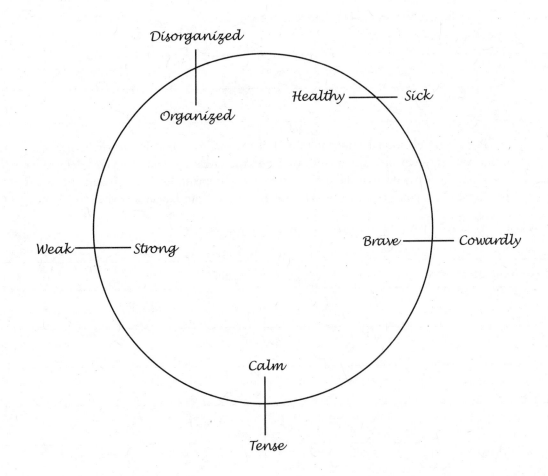

Chapter 6—Day Two cont.

a. How do the qualities *inside* the circle make you feel?

_____

_____

_____

b. How do the qualities *outside* the circle make you feel?

_____

_____

_____

A negative emotional response to any of the qualities outside the circle means the qualities inside are requirements. The qualities outside the circle are your triggers. Remember, a trigger is an event or thought that doesn't meet your requirement, and your requirement activates your I-System. Once your requirement is defused, there it is no longer a trigger.

c. List your requirements and triggers about how you want to be:

Requirement	Trigger

d. Can you ever do enough to meet the requirements inside the circle? No. Once a belief is a requirement, enough is never enough, and you end up with never-ending negative self-beliefs.

DAY THREE   DATE: _____

1. During the day, what requirements for yourself were you able to defuse?

Requirement	How did you defuse it?	What happened?
I should always be in control of my life.	Did a Problem map about losing control with my son, saw how my requirement caused most of my distress.	I talked calmly to my son at dinner and could then listen to him without overeating or stressing out.

Your I-System drives you to believe you are just a bagful of requirements.

2. List your requirements for yourself that you continue to struggle with:

_____

_____

_____

_____

_____

   Please note that mind-body bridging is a gentle, step-by-step process, and each step frees your ability to heal yourself. You're starting to experience yourself as much greater than who you thought you were.

Chapter 6—Day Three cont.

3. Do a My Most Troubling Requirement for Myself map. Choose the requirement you are having the most trouble with from the previous list and write it in the following oval. Take several minutes to write your thoughts outside the oval. Work quickly, without editing your thoughts. Describe your body tension at the bottom of the map.

MY MOST TROUBLING REQUIREMENT FOR MYSELF MAP

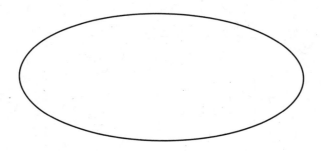

Body Tension:

_____

_____

a. Is your mind cluttered or clear?

_____

b. List your requirements:

_____

_____

_____

c. Are any of the items on the map related to your traumatic event? Yes _____ No _____

Chapter 6—Day Three cont.

4. Do the map again, writing the same requirement in the oval. Before you continue writing, listen to background sounds, feel your body's pressure on your seat, sense your feet on the floor, and feel the pen in your hand. Once you're settled, keep feeling the pen in your hand and write any thoughts that come to mind. As you write, keep paying attention to background sounds, feeling the pen in your hand, and watching the ink go onto the paper. Write for several minutes.

MY MOST TROUBLING REQUIREMENT
FOR MYSELF MAP WITH BRIDGING

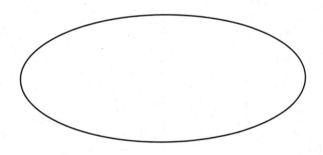

a. How is this map different from the previous one?

_____

_____

_____

b. How would your life be different if the mind-body state you had while doing this map were present every day?

_____

_____

_____

DAY FOUR   DATE: _____

Notice how negative thoughts about your trauma are used by your depressor, spun into storylines, and embedded into your body. Over time, this negative self-talk turns into the mind-body belief that you are damaged. This is a negative self-belief, a dysfunctional mind-body state filled with negative thoughts about your traumatic experience.

1.   During the day, notice any negative self-beliefs related to your trauma. What was the impact on your life?

Negative Self-Belief	Storylines	Body Tension	Impact on Your Life or How You Behaved
I'll always have PTSD.	It happened so fast, I can't believe it happened to me. I'll never be the same...	Chest tight, band around head	Can't keep a job. Kids stay away from me. I avoid people.

2.   List three negative self-beliefs about your traumatic event:

_____

_____

_____

Chapter 6—Day Four cont.

a. In the oval, write the most troubling negative self-belief from your list. Around the oval, jot your thoughts quickly, without editing them. Describe your body tension at the bottom of the map. If needed, see the sample map that follows.

MY MOST TROUBLING NEGATIVE SELF-BELIEF MAP

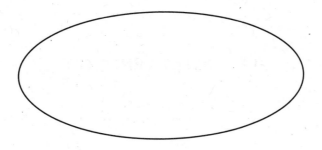

Body Tension:

_____

_____

Fill out this chart using the info on your map:

Depressors	Fixers	Storylines	Requirements
I'm useless.	Try harder.	The trauma was too much. Why did it happen to me?	I should have done more. I should be strong enough to get over it.

The My Most Troubling Negative Self-Belief map shows how your I-System captures natural thoughts about your traumatic event, and how the depressor and fixer then create storylines that embed negativity in every cell of your body, disrupting your life. Your I-System's requirements keep this vicious cycle going, but defusing your requirements lets you break the cycle.

Chapter 6—Day Four cont.

SAMPLE MAP:
MY MOST TROUBLING NEGATIVE SELF-BELIEF

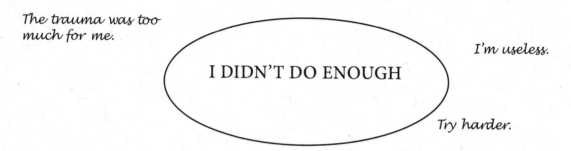

I should have done more.

My life is too hard.

The trauma was too much for me.

I DIDN'T DO ENOUGH

I'm useless.

Try harder.

I brought it on myself.

I should be strong enough to get over it.

Why did it happen to me?

Chapter 6—Day Four cont.

3. Do the map again, writing the same negative self-belief in the oval. Before you continue writing, listen to background sounds, feel your body's pressure on your seat, sense your feet on the floor, and feel the pen in your hand. Once you're settled, keep feeling the pen in your hand, and start writing any thoughts that come to mind about that belief. As you write, keep paying attention to background sounds, feeling the pen in your hand, and watching the ink go onto the paper.

MY MOST TROUBLING NEGATIVE SELF-BELIEF MAP WITH BRIDGING

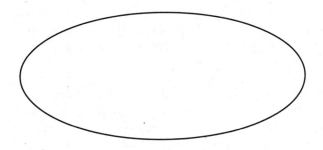

    a. How is this map different from the previous one?

_____

_____

    b. List the requirements from your previous map that you feel you can defuse:

_____

_____

    c. List the requirements from your previous map that you feel will be difficult to defuse:

_____

_____

    d. Use your bridging awareness practices and thought labeling on these requirements and notice if the tension lessens. What happens?

_____

_____

DAY FIVE   DATE: _____

Healing Negative Self Beliefs

Let's review your mind-body bridging tools for healing negative self-beliefs related to your trauma:

- *Bridging awareness practices*—When you notice negative self-talk and body tension related to your traumatic event, recognize it as a sign of an overactive I-System, tune in to your senses, and then mindfully return to what you were doing.

- *Thought labeling*—When a negative thought pops into your mind, remember, a thought is just a thought. Label your negative thoughts as mere thoughts, and return to what you were doing. For example, when *I'll never be the same* pops into your mind, say to yourself, *I'm having the thought "I'll never be the same," and it's just a thought.*

- *Storyline awareness*—When you catch yourself mulling over stories about negative self-beliefs, notice the repetitive themes, recognize them as storylines, and return to the task at hand. It doesn't matter if the stories are true or false, positive or negative. Remember, it's not your negative thoughts that get you down or your positive thoughts that pull you up; your storylines create mind clutter and fill every cell of your body with tension, supporting the depressor-fixer cycle. Your I-System's capturing of stories is what takes you away from the present.

- *Mapping*—Use the mind-body bridging maps. The first map helps you find your requirements about negative self-beliefs related to your trauma. Noticing your body tension is what helps you find these requirements. Use your bridging awareness practices on the second map to see the truth about negative self-beliefs and return to your natural functioning true self.

- *Defusing requirements*—When you notice body tension and negative self-talk, take a moment to use your mind-body bridging tools to identify your requirement (for example, if you notice the self-talk *I'll never be the same*, you might find that the requirement is *I should be just as I was before*). Remember, your current distress is from an overactive I-System, not past events. Staying aware of your requirement as it comes up in real time reduces its power. You will know you have defused the requirement when you notice sudden or gradual release of body tension.

Chapter 6—Day Five cont.

1. During the day, use your mind-body bridging tools to keep negative self-talk and self-beliefs from getting you down and interfering with your life.
What happened?

Negative Self-Belief	Body Tension	How You Used Your Mind-Body Bridging Tools	Body Sensations	How Your Behavior Changed After Bridging
I'll never be the same.	Chest tight, shallow breath	Labeled my thoughts Listened to hum of air conditioner	Chest and breathing relaxed	Got more done Wasn't as depressed
I could have done more.	Gut cramps	I immediately recognized the thought "I should have done more" as a requirement	Calmer	"Light came on," day went smoothly

It's not your trauma that's interfering with your life; it's your requirements that keep the past from becoming the past. It's impossible for negative self-beliefs to keep going when the I-System is quiet. Negative self-beliefs mean your requirements are disconnecting you from your self-healing power. You are starting to see that no matter what you went through in the past, your mind-body bridging practices can change your life.

2. Do a map using your most persistent negative self-belief related to your trauma. Write it in the oval, and around the oval jot your thoughts about that negative self-belief. Work quickly, without editing your thoughts. Describe your body tension at the bottom of the map.

MOST PERSISTENT NEGATIVE SELF-BELIEF ABOUT MY TRAUMA MAP

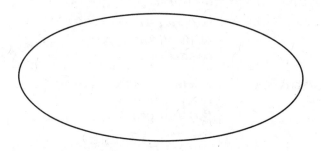

Body Tension:

_____

_____

a. What are your depressors?

_____

b. What are your fixers?

_____

c. What are your storylines?

_____

d. For each thought on your map, find and list the underlying requirement (for example, if you thought, *It will never be over*, the requirement might be *I should be over it by now*).

_____

These requirements activate the I-System, recycle your trauma, and prevent healing. Remember, it's not the event that's the problem; it's the requirements. Recognizing and defusing your requirements creates space for you to heal yourself.

Chapter 6—Day Five cont.

3. Do the map again, writing the same negative self-belief in the oval. Before you continue writing, listen to background sounds, feel your body's pressure on your seat, sense your feet on the floor, and feel the pen in your hand. Once you're settled, keep feeling the pen in your hand, and start writing any thoughts that come to mind about that self-belief. As you write, keep paying attention to background sounds, feeling the pen in your hand, and watching the ink go onto the paper.

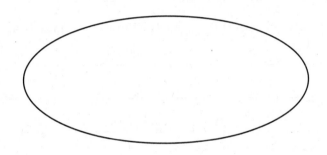

> ## MOST PERSISTENT NEGATIVE SELF-BELIEF
> ## ABOUT MY TRAUMA MAP WITH BRIDGING

    a.   How is this map different from the previous one?

_____

    b.   How would you live your life in this state?

_____

_____

You are starting to realize that it's your requirements about the trauma that activate your I-System, not your negative thoughts. Using bridging maps shows you the power of mind-body bridging practices. You've also begun to see the effect of your self-healing powers on your PTSD symptoms.

DAY SIX   DATE: _____

Your success in healing negative self-beliefs related to your trauma is dependent on your ability to defuse requirements for yourself.

1. Notice whatever success you have with defusing requirements throughout your day:

    a. How long does negative self-talk go on before you can recognize that your I-System is active?

    _____

    _____

    _____

    _____

    Do you recognize the requirements that are related to your trauma? If so, list them:

    _____

    _____

    _____

    _____

    How can you defuse them?

    _____

    _____

    _____

    _____

    b. For those negative self-beliefs that continue, it's helpful to repeat the Most Persistent Negative Self-Belief About My Trauma maps on a separate piece of paper.

Chapter 6—Day Six cont.

2. Do a Where I Should Be in My Healing Process map. Around the oval, jot any thoughts that come to mind. Work quickly, without editing your thoughts. List your body tensions at the bottom of the map.

WHERE I SHOULD
BE IN MY HEALING
PROCESS

Body Tension:

_____

_____

Looking at the info on your map, fill out this chart:

Depressors	Fixers	Storylines	Requirements

3. Do this map again using your bridging awareness practices. Before you start writing, listen to background sounds, feel your body's pressure on your seat, sense your feet on the floor, and feel the pen in your hand. Once you're settled, keep feeling the pen in your hand, and start writing any thoughts that come to mind. As you write, keep paying attention to background sounds and feeling the pen in your hand, as you watch the ink go onto the paper. Write for several minutes.

```
      ⸺⸺⸺⸺⸺⸺⸺
    ╱                     ╲
   ╱   WHERE I SHOULD      ╲
  │    BE IN MY HEALING     │
   ╲  PROCESS WITH BRIDGING╱
    ╲                     ╱
      ⸺⸺⸺⸺⸺⸺⸺
```

a. How is this map different from the previous one?

_____

_____

b. This map shows you that you function naturally when your I-System is calm. What do you notice about your sense of self-worth? Are you healing and connecting to your inner wisdom?

_____

_____

_____

_____

Use your mind-body bridging practices in your daily life, being gentle with yourself and noticing what happens. Your life is a series of moment-by-moment events, and when you befriend your I-System, you are in the driver's seat.

DAY SEVEN   DATE: _____

Each moment of your life is a presentation. Today, using your mind-body bridging practices, discover who is presenting: your damaged self or your true self? Observe your presentations today.

1. *Damaged self*—List five situations where your I-System was overactive:

_____

_____

_____

_____

_____

_____

2. *True self*—List five situations where your I-System was calm:

_____

_____

_____

_____

_____

_____

3. Can your negative self-beliefs related to your trauma exist when your I-System is at rest?
   Yes ____   No ____

Chapter 6—Day Seven cont.

4. Do a Who Am I? map. Inside the circle, write the qualities that best describe who you are. After you have listed at least six qualities, outside the circle write the opposite of each quality and connect it with a line. If needed, see the sample map that follows.

WHO AM I? MAP

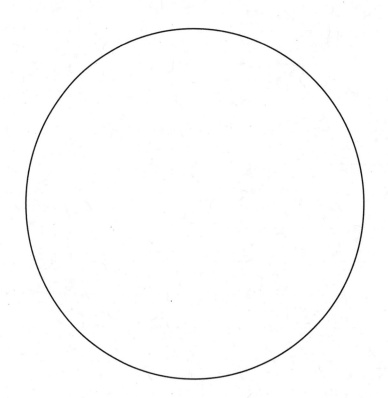

Chapter 6—Day Seven cont.

SAMPLE MAP: WHO AM I?

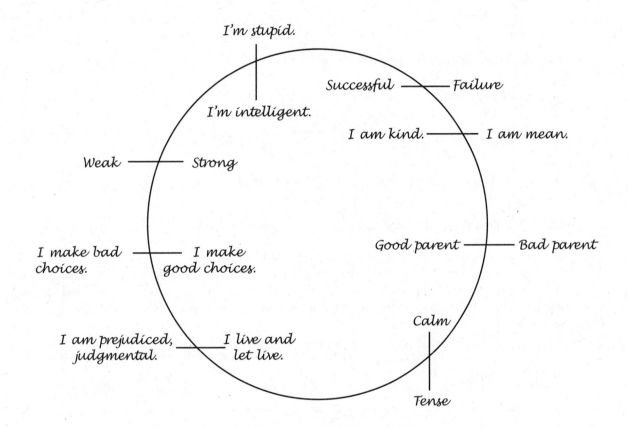

Chapter 6—Day Seven cont.

    a.   How does each quality inside the circle make you feel?

_____

_____

_____

_____

    b.   How does each quality outside the circle make you feel?

_____

_____

_____

_____

    c.   Do the qualities inside the circle really describe who you are? Yes _____ No _____

    d.   Do the qualities outside the circle really describe who you are? Yes _____ No _____

           Your I-System has you believing that the qualities inside the circle define you. Whenever you think you have any of the qualities outside the circle, your I-System tells you you're lacking or damaged. Your I-System wants to convince you that you are who you *think* you are. The qualities you listed are just thoughts, not you.

    e.   Using bridging awareness practices and thought labeling, review all the qualities on your map. What happens?

_____

_____

_____

_____

        With bridging, you expand the circle to include everything on your map. When you aren't driven by your requirements, you are *everything*, which means you can have any quality on your map (even negative ones) without activating your I-System.

MBB WEEKLY EVALUATION SCALE
HEAL THE NEGATIVE SELF-BELIEFS TRAUMA CAUSES

Date: _____

During the past week, how did you do with these practices? Check the description that best matches your practice: hardly ever, occasionally, usually, or almost always.

How often do you...	Hardly Ever	Occasionally	Usually	Almost Always
Realize that requirements always activate your I-System and impair your healing and functioning?				
Realize that requirements keep your negative self-beliefs going?				
Keep from getting upset by defusing a requirement?				
See that your requirements for yourself trap you and keep you from being who you really are?				
Experience yourself as far more than who you thought you were?				
Experience that all you need to do to act from your true self is quiet your I-System so that natural functioning follows?				
Recognize your damaged self?				
Experience your damaged self as a myth of the I-System?				
Recognize natural functioning?				
Appreciate your true self, who you are when you function naturally moment by moment?				
Appreciate parts of everyday life in a new light?				
Experience yourself as connected to a wellspring of healing, goodness, and wisdom?				
Notice that your relationships have improved?				
Function better at home and at work?				
Notice a decrease in negative self-beliefs?				

List three requirements that used to cause you to have a meltdown and that you now deal with by releasing the I-System's tension and letting yourself function naturally:

_____

_____

_____

CHAPTER 7

RESOLVE TRAUMA
MEMORIES STEP BY STEP

Completing the exercises in the previous chapters has prepared you for today. You've learned tools to quiet and befriend your I-System, building the foundation to tackle your trauma experience. When your I-System is overactive, creating chaos, it may feel like a foe. But you have also come to see it as a friend who alerts you whenever you veer off course from your true self. Now, recognizing early signs of an overactive I-System, using bridging awareness practices, befriending your depressor and fixer, and defusing your requirements are everyday activities. Sometimes your mind-body bridging practices are effortless, and sometimes they take lots of effort; natural functioning can be either way, and natural functioning is what you're doing more and more of.

To resolve trauma memories, you'll do a lot of mind-body mapping, which, as you know, is the quick, simple practice of freely jotting your thoughts on paper and noting your body sensations. Mapping gives your naturally functioning awareness the chance to gently notice your active I-System. This chapter introduces an advanced mapping practice called *bubble mapping*, a simple and powerful tool that adds more clarity and reduces your I-System's emotional distortion.

DAY ONE   DATE: _____

1. Recall the symptoms related to your trauma that bothered you before you started this workbook. Log those symptoms in the chart below and compare how they were used at the start with how they are now. This list of symptoms might help:

    ◆ Having flashbacks—intrusive thoughts, smells, pictures, sounds, sensations, or feelings that pop into your mind about your trauma, as if you were reliving your trauma

    ◆ Having flashbacks so intense and powerful that you lose track of where you are

    ◆ Having nightmares—intense, startling bad dreams—related to the trauma

    ◆ Avoiding situations, thoughts, or feelings related to the trauma

    ◆ Feeling numb or unemotional

    ◆ Being uninterested in the world around you

    ◆ Being in an overstimulated mind-body state (increased arousal, revved up) that results in trouble sleeping or concentrating, irritability, anger, being on guard or easily startled, and restlessness

    After logging your symptoms in this chart, rate their frequency as *never*, *weekly*, *2–3x week*, or *daily*; and rate their effect on your life as *none*, *mild*, *moderate*, or *severe*:

	Before Workbook		Present	
Symptom	**Frequency**	**Impact on life**	**Frequency**	**Impact on life**
Intrusive thoughts about accident and death	*daily*	*severe*	*weekly*	*mild*

Chapter 7—Day One cont.

2. Do a Trauma map by writing your most troubling memory of your traumatic event in the oval. Around the oval, scatter your thoughts about the event, writing for three to five minutes. Describe your body tension at the bottom of the map. See the two sample maps on page 150.

TRAUMA MAP

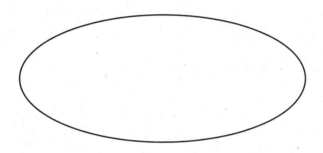

Body Tension:

_____

_____

a. *Bubble* your map by drawing a circle (bubble) around a thought that brings a lot of body tension. Take a few minutes to scatter your thoughts around the circled thought. Now bubble a second troubling thought.

b. List below your requirements for the thoughts that are around each bubble. (For example, in sample map B, the thought *People shouldn't stare at me* is both a thought and a require-ment, and the thought *I hate to go out in public* has the hidden requirement *I shouldn't go out in public*).

_____

_____

_____

_____

SAMPLE MAP A: TRAUMA BUBBLE

He was my
responsibility.

I should
have done
more.

Can't sleep.

John was
killed

I'll never
get over it.

He was like a
brother.

Getting
Ambushed

Why didn't we know?

We should have had
better intelligence.

Everything is upside down.

Can't keep track

Can't tell
who the
enemy is

Hate going
in crowds

Those sudden
movements

On guard

SAMPLE MAP B: TRAUMA BUBBLE

People shouldn't stare at me.

Why did I wear that dress?

I hate to go out in public.

The way they look at me

Most places are dangerous.

Everyone knows.

I'm horrible.

Being attacked and raped

Can't sleep

God doesn't love me.

I shouldn't have walked down that street.

Why did I drink so much?

Why didn't I act faster?

I should have known by how he acted.

I should have left.

Chapter 7—Day One cont.

3. Take one of the bubble items from your Trauma map and write it in the following oval (for example, *The way they look at me*). Before you continue writing, listen to background sounds, feel your body's pressure on your seat, sense your feet on the floor, and feel the pen in your hand. Once you're settled, keep feeling the pen in your hand, and start writing. Watch the ink go onto the paper and listen to background sounds. For the next few minutes, jot any thoughts that come to mind.

FIRST BUBBLE TRAUMA MAP WITH BRIDGING

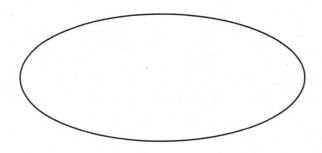

Compare the body tension on this map with that on your earlier trauma map:

_____

_____

_____

This mapping experience shows you your ability to heal yourself.

Chapter 7—Day One cont.

4. Take the other bubble item from your Trauma map and write it in the oval (for example, *Why didn't I act faster?*). Before you continue writing, listen to background sounds and feel your body's pressure on your seat, your feet on the floor, and the pen in your hand. Once you're settled, keep feeling the pen in your hand and start writing. Watch the ink go onto the paper and listen to background sounds. For the next few minutes, jot any thoughts that come to mind.

SECOND BUBBLE TRAUMA MAP WITH BRIDGING

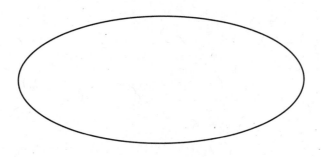

Compare the body tension on this map with that on your earlier Trauma map:

_____

_____

_____

Chapter 7—Day One cont.

5. Now do today's first Trauma map exercise again. In the oval below, write the same traumatic event you mapped the first time. Before you start writing, listen to background sounds and feel your body's pressure on your seat, your feet on the floor, and the pen in your hand. Once you're settled, keep feeling the pen in your hand as you start writing. Watch the ink go onto the paper and listen to background sounds. For the next few minutes, jot any thoughts that come to mind.

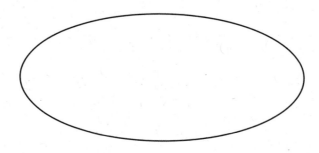

TRAUMA MAP WITH BRIDGING

Compare this map to your first trauma map. What do you notice?

_____

_____

_____

On your first trauma map, through the lens of your I-System, you experienced your trauma memories. On this bridging map you experienced your trauma memories again, but with a quiet I-System and through the lens of your true self. Mind-body bridging lets you see the truth about your traumatic event without your overactive I-System's distortions.

6. Go over the first Trauma map from today's exercise, and note items that bring body tension. Recognize the underlying requirement.

Item that Causes Body Tension	Requirement
Why did I wear that dress? Those sudden movements	I shouldn't have worn that dress. There shouldn't be sudden movements.

7. Do you see that the way you experience your trauma memories again and again depends solely on the I-System's overactivity, which uses thoughts and memories of your traumatic event to keep itself going? Yes _____ No _____

    As you know, only requirements can activate your I-System. Resolving trauma memories and healing yourself happen when you identify and defuse requirements related to both your current situation (for example, *There shouldn't be sudden movements*) and your past traumatic event (for example, *I shouldn't have worn that dress*).

8. Describe how you are going to defuse the previous requirements in real time:

_____

_____

_____

_____

_____

DAY TWO   DATE: _____

During the day, be aware of when you are experiencing your trauma memories, and reduce your mind-body distress by quieting your I-System (using bridging awareness practices and thought labeling, and recognizing and defusing requirements).

1. What happened?

_____

_____

_____

_____

_____

_____

_____

2. Who is experiencing your trauma memories, the true self or the damaged self? What did you observe?

_____

_____

_____

_____

_____

_____

Your true self (who you are with a quiet I-System) has so much space (review figure 1.1) that any memory you have won't interfere with your life.

Chapter 7—Day Two cont.

3. Do a Trauma map about a traumatic memory that keeps coming back again and again. Write the memory of the traumatic event in the oval. Around the oval, scatter your thoughts about that event for three to four minutes. Then note your body tension at the bottom of the map.

TRAUMA MAP

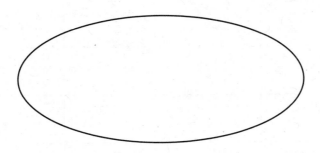

Body Tension:

_____

_____

4. Bubble your map by drawing a circle (bubble) around the thought that brings excess body tension. Take a few minutes to scatter your thoughts around the circled item. Bubble any other troubling items.

Chapter 7—Day Two cont.

a. Fill out the following log using your bubbled map. List any body tension related to each item. Identify the underlying requirements.

Item	Body Tension	Requirement

b. Review the previous list using your bridging awareness practices and thought labeling. Take your time. There's nothing to fix. Your awareness is all it takes to gently heal.

Continue using your mind-body bridging practices for the rest of the day to quiet your I-System and defuse your requirements, which are the source of your troubling symptoms.

Chapter 7—Day Two cont.

5. Do the last Trauma map again. Write the same memory of the traumatic event in the oval. Before you start writing, listen to background sounds and feel your body's pressure on your seat, your feet on the floor, and the pen in your hand. Once you are settled, keep feeling the pen in your hand as you start writing. Watch the ink go onto the paper and listen to background sounds. For the next few minutes, jot any thoughts that come to mind.

TRAUMA MAP WITH BRIDGING

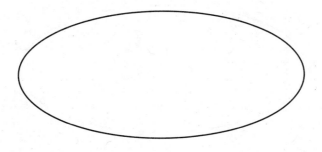

Notice the differences between the two maps:

a. What's your mind-body state after bridging?

_____

_____

_____

b. Do you see the truth that no matter who you are or what you've been through, you have the power and wisdom to heal yourself? Yes _____ No _____

c. Can you defuse your requirements from the previous map when the situation arises again? Yes _____ No _____

DAY THREE   DATE: _____

1. Do a Nightmare map. In the oval, write your bad dream's most disturbing image, theme, or content. Around the oval, scatter any thoughts that pop into your mind. Don't be concerned if the thoughts seem unrelated to the nightmare. Take your time. When you're done, write about your body tension at the bottom of the map.

```
┌─────────────────────────────────────────────────────┐
│                   NIGHTMARE MAP                       │
└─────────────────────────────────────────────────────┘
```

Body Tension:

_____

_____

Dreaming is an organizing and processing function that's vital to your well-being. Its purpose is to heal and refresh your mental and physical health. Your biological system supplies the hardware for dreams, and your I-System is the primary supplier of the software or content. Why? Because dreaming tries to resolve your spinning thoughts. As you already know, the I-System is the main producer of these spinning thoughts, so most of the content of dreams relates to the I-System.

Chapter 7—Day Three cont.

2. On your map, see if you can find these signs of your I-System:

   a. What are your depressors?

   _____

   _____

   _____

   _____

   b. What are your fixers?

   _____

   _____

   _____

   _____

   c. What are your storylines?

   _____

   _____

   _____

   _____

   d. What are your underlying requirements?

   _____

   _____

   _____

   _____

3. Do the Nightmare map again. In the oval, write the same disturbing image, theme, or content from your bad dream. Before you start writing, listen to background sounds and feel your body's pressure on your seat, your feet on the floor, and the pen in your hand. Once you are settled, keep feeling the pen in your hand as you start writing. Watch the ink go onto the paper and listen to background sounds. For the next few minutes, jot any thoughts that come to mind.

NIGHTMARE MAP WITH BRIDGING

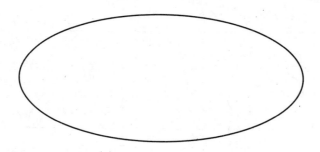

    a. Compare your two maps:

_____

_____

_____

_____

    b. Are you starting to realize that the I-System is mainly responsible for your nightmares? Yes _____ No _____

Mind-Body Bridging Tools for Better Sleep

1. Before bed, do a What's on My Mind map. In the middle of a piece of paper, write "What's on My Mind" and draw an oval around it. Next, jot whatever thoughts come to mind. Remember, the busy head can never settle the busy head. Note your I-System's unresolved activity. Now do the map again using your bridging awareness practices. With a quiet I-System, you are ready to sleep.

2. In bed, make a habit of using your favorite nighttime bridging awareness practice (for example, listen to the fan or the clock's ticking; feel the texture of the blanket, pillow, or sheets).

3. If you wake up for any reason, notice your requirements, such as *I shouldn't wake up in the middle of the night*, *The dog shouldn't bark*, or *The neighbors should be quiet*. Use your bridging awareness practices before your storylines gain traction.

4. If you have nightmares or bad dreams, notice any obvious requirements, such as *I shouldn't have bad dreams or nightmares*, realize that the force behind your bad dream is not the horrendous content but your overactive I-System, and go back to your bridging awareness practice.

5. On mornings after you've had bad dreams or nightmares, do a Bad Dream/Nightmare map. On a piece of paper, write your bad dream's most disturbing image, theme, or content. Draw an oval around it. Around the oval, scatter your thoughts quickly, without editing them. Pay special attention to your depressors and fixers, and recognize as many requirements as you can. The I-System wants you to search for your dream's meaning and create more storylines, rather than see the dream as the I-System's creation. Now do the map again using your bridging awareness practices. This second map (the bridging awareness map) lets you release the dream's energy, pain, and power.

Making a habit of using your daytime mind-body bridging practices calms your I-System so that your mind-body can regulate and heal itself. Gradually, your sleep will improve, and you'll wake up refreshed.

DAY FOUR   DATE: _____

1. Throughout the day, be aware of when you want to avoid activities, places, people, or events. Log what or whom you avoid, noting whether you can find an underlying traumatic event.

What or Whom I Avoid	Traumatic Event
Driving on freeways	My child died in an accident while I was driving
Dating men	Raped by an ex-boyfriend
Riding on the subway	(Don't know)
Going to VA hospital	Combat in Iraq

Chapter 7—Day Four cont.

2. Do a map about the activity, place, person, or event you try to avoid the most that's related to the traumatic event. Write it in the oval. Around the oval, scatter your thoughts for three to five minutes, without editing them. Write your body tension at the bottom of the map. See the sample maps on page 166.

WHAT OR WHOM I AVOID MAP

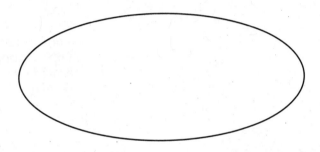

Body Tension:

_____

_____

   a. Bubble your map by drawing a circle (bubble) around the item that brings the most body tension. Take a few minutes to scatter your thoughts around the circled item. Bubble any other troubling items.

   b. Identify and list as many requirements as possible:

_____

_____

   c. How do you act in this state?

_____

SAMPLE MAP A: WHAT OR WHOM I AVOID

They drive like
they're drunk.

All that construction

Death trap

Maybe I'm crazy.

*Driving
on
Freeways*

Nobody cares.

Accidents
everywhere

People drive crazy.

They don't pay
attention.

Body Tension:
Tight chest
Hard to breathe

Requirements:
People shouldn't drive crazy.
Shouldn't be construction.
Freeways should be safe.

SAMPLE MAP B: WHAT OR WHOM I AVOID

He will never
like me when
he finds out.

He might hurt me.

I'm dirty.

He wants to go
out with me.

He's attractive.

*Dating
a man*

I'm terrified.

I'm weak.

It's not safe.

It will end up bad.

Body Tension:
Shoulders pulled up
Stomach aches

Requirements:
He shouldn't hurt me.
It should be safe.
I should be strong.

Chapter 7—Day Four cont.

3. Do the What or Whom I Avoid map again. Write the same activity, place, person, or event in the oval. Before you start writing, listen to background sounds and feel your body's pressure on your seat, your feet on the floor, and the pen in your hand. Once you are settled, keep feeling the pen in your hand as you start writing. Watch the ink go onto the paper and listen to background sounds. For the next few minutes, jot any thoughts that come to mind.

WHAT OR WHOM I AVOID MAP WITH BRIDGING

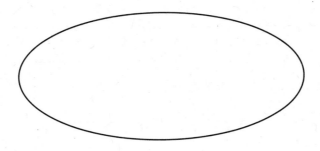

Notice the differences between the two maps:

a. What's your mind-body state after bridging?

_____

_____

By bridging, this map shows you that your need to avoid people and situations relates directly to your I-System. When your I-System is overactive, you give up your freedom of choice. With a calm I-System, your past trauma doesn't limit your choices of whom to interact with, where to go, or what activities to engage in.

b. Now can you defuse your requirements from the previous map when the situation comes up again and take back your freedom of choice? Yes _____ No _____

DAY FIVE   DATE: _____

1. During the day, whenever you are emotionally numb, take a moment to tune in to your senses and then go back to what you were doing.

    a.   When you tuned in to your senses, what happened?

    _____

    _____

    _____

    b.   Were there events that triggered your I-System and caused you to go numb? If so, list them:

    _____

    _____

    _____

    c.   Can you identify the underlying requirements?

    _____

    _____

    _____

    d.   How did you defuse the requirements?

    _____

    _____

    _____

    Whenever unwanted emotions come up, it's important to recognize the underlying requirement that causes you to go numb (for example, *I don't want to feel this or think about that*). Using your bridging awareness practices lets you see that you are far more than your past traumatic event and the feelings you want to avoid. Making a habit of using your bridging awareness practices is important to feeling alive again.

Chapter 7—Day Five cont.

2. Do an Emotion map. In the oval, write the emotion that's affecting your life the most (for example, anger, rage, sadness, or numbness). Around the oval, scatter your thoughts for three to five minutes, without editing them. Write about your body tension at the bottom of the map.

EMOTION MAP

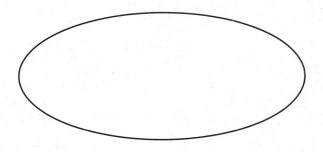

Body Tension:

_____

_____

a. Bubble your map, drawing a circle (bubble) around the thought that brings lots of body tension. Take a few minutes to scatter more thoughts around the circled item. Bubble any other troubling items.

b. Identify and list as many requirements as possible:

_____

_____

_____

c. How do you act in this state?

_____

Chapter 7—Day Five cont.

3. Do the map again, writing the same emotion in the oval. Before you start writing, listen to background sounds and feel your body's pressure on your seat, your feet on the floor, and the pen in your hand. Once you are settled, keep feeling the pen in your hand as you start writing. Watch the ink go onto the paper and listen to background sounds. For the next few minutes, jot any thoughts that come to mind.

EMOTION MAP WITH BRIDGING

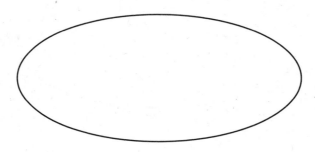

What's your mind-body state after bridging, and how do you act in this state?

_____

_____

_____

Like thoughts, all emotions are from natural functioning until the I-System captures them. During the day, when your emotions seem to be getting the best of you, use your bridging awareness practices and thought labeling to recognize two parts of emotions: thoughts and body sensations. As you learned from this map, emotions can't take the driver's seat away from your true self when your body is calm. Try it right now. Stir up a troubling emotional situation, listen to background sounds, and notice what happens to your body. To take over control, your I-System needs your body to be tense.

DAY SIX   DATE: _____

1. Jot the three biggest things holding you back in your life. Do they include your looks, brains, kids, lack of money, poor education, race, trauma, or something else?

    _____

    _____

2. Do a What's Holding Me Back map. In the oval, write the biggest thing that's currently holding you back. Around the oval, scatter your thoughts for three to five minutes, without editing them. Write your body tension at the bottom of the map.

WHAT'S HOLDING ME BACK MAP

Body Tension:

_____

_____

a. List your storylines:

_____

b. List your requirements:

_____

c. How do you act in this state?

_____

3. Do this map again. In the oval, write the same problem that's holding you back. Before you start writing, listen to background sounds and feel your body's pressure on your seat, your feet on the floor, and the pen in your hand. Once you are settled, keep feeling the pen in your hand as you start writing. Watch the ink go onto the paper and listen to background sounds. For the next few minutes, jot any thoughts that come to mind.

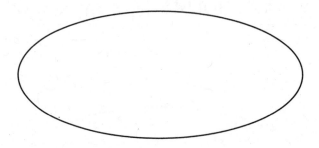

| WHAT'S HOLDING ME BACK MAP WITH BRIDGING |

a. What's your mind-body state after bridging?

_____

_____

b. Are the things on your previous map what's really holding you back, or is it your listed requirements?

_____

_____

c. Can you see new options on this map that will let you move forward with your life? List them:

_____

_____

_____

DAY SEVEN   DATE: _____

1. Today, if you feel irritable, angry, on guard, or easily startled, or if you're having a tough time concentrating, take a moment to tune in to your senses and use your favorite mind-body bridging tools.

    a. List the situations. How did it go?

    _____

    _____

    _____

    _____

    _____

    b. Did you recognize your underlying requirements? If so, list them:

    _____

    _____

    _____

    _____

    c. Do you see that your I-System, activated by your requirements, causes your distress, limitations, and troubling behaviors? Yes _____ No _____

    d. Can you experience yourself as not being incomplete or damaged? Yes _____ No _____

2. List any of the previous situations that still causes distress even when you use your mind-body bridging tools:

    _____

    _____

    _____

    _____

Chapter 7—Day Seven cont.

3. Do a map using the most troubling situation from the previous list. Write it in the oval, and scatter your thoughts around it for three to five minutes, without editing them. Write your body tension at the bottom of the map.

SITUATION STILL CAUSING DISTRESS MAP

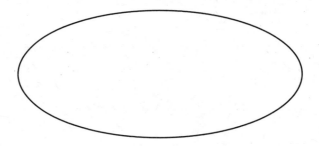

Body Tension:

_____

_____

a. Bubble your map, drawing a circle (bubble) around the thought that brings the most body tension. Take a few minutes to scatter more thoughts around the circled item. Bubble any other troubling items.

b. Identify as many requirements as possible:

_____

_____

_____

_____

c. How do you act in this state?

_____

Chapter 7—Day Seven cont.

4. Do the map again, writing the same situation in the oval. Before you start writing, listen to background sounds and feel your body's pressure on your seat, your feet on the floor, and the pen in your hand. Once you are settled, keep feeling the pen in your hand as you start writing. Watch the ink go onto the paper and listen to background sounds. For the next few minutes, jot any thoughts that come to mind.

SITUATION STILL CAUSING DISTRESS MAP WITH BRIDGING

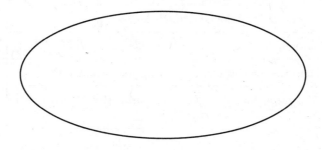

   a.   What's your mind-body state now?

_____

_____

   b.   Write how you will be better able to deal with that situation when it comes up again:

_____

_____

_____

5. Go back to your symptom log from Day One at the start of this chapter. On a separate sheet of paper, map any symptoms you still have. Remember, use all your bridging tools (bridging awareness practices, thought labeling, and recognizing and defusing requirements). Watch the symptoms lose the power they once had.

MBB WEEKLY EVALUATION SCALE
RESOLVE TRAUMA MEMORIES STEP BY STEP

Date: _____

During the past week, how did you do with these practices? Check the description that best matches your practice: hardly ever, occasionally, usually, or almost always.

How often do you...	Hardly Ever	Occasionally	Usually	Almost Always
See that trauma memories create body tension and mind clutter?				
Notice when your I-System captures trauma memories, disrupting your life?				
Recognize requirements about past traumas that are causing your symptoms?				
During the day, get beneficial effects from defusing requirements that triggered your I-System?				
Keep your I-System from activating so that you don't have to relive trauma memories?				
Use mind-body bridging practices to feel connected to your body and everyday activities?				
Sleep, relax, and concentrate better, and notice that you have a more-even disposition?				

List three requirements you have defused:

_____

_____

_____

List three examples of how your life has changed from using mind-body bridging:

_____

_____

_____

_____

DEALING WITH YOUR TRAUMA: TRIGGERS AND FEARS

This chapter focuses on trauma-related triggers and fears that hold you back from healing yourself. You'll realize it's not your current activities, the past traumatic event, or even your memories of your trauma that are causing your distress. It's your current requirements, which activate your I-System, supporting your false belief that you are incomplete and damaged.

Triggers are current events that fail to meet your requirements, activating your I-System. Once activated, your I-System spins storylines (memories of past trauma, in this case) to create mind-body distress. When you become aware of a trigger (for example, a sound, a smell, or something someone says or does), it's important to understand that it's directing you to the real culprit, your requirement. In this chapter, you will have the chance to see for yourself that you're not a victim of your fears, limitations, or past traumatic events. Your mind-body can heal from PTSD, and peace of mind is within your grasp.

DAY ONE   DATE: _____

1. An event or thought can trigger the I-System only if it fails to meet one of your requirements. Throughout the day, notice any events that distress you because they remind you of a past trauma. Note any body tension the events bring up. Log your experiences.

Current Trigger	Requirement Not Met	My Reaction	Traumatic Event
Helicopter sounds	Helicopters should not fly around my house.	Tight chest, clenched fist, rapid heartbeat, want to run for cover	Combat

Remember, it's not the current event or trigger that causes your distress; it's the failure to meet your requirement that activates your I-System.

Chapter 8—Day One cont.

2. Do a Trigger map. Choose a triggering event from the previous chart. Write it in the oval. Next, around the oval, scatter any thoughts that come to mind. Write for three to five minutes, without editing your thoughts. Describe your body tension at the bottom of the map.

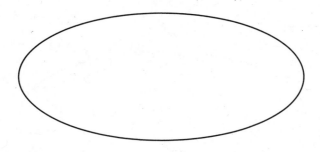

TRIGGER MAP

Body Tension:

_____

_____

   a. Bubble your map by drawing a circle (bubble) around the thought that brings the most body tension. Take a few minutes to scatter more thoughts around the circled item. Bubble any other troubling items.

   b. List your requirements:

_____

_____

_____

_____

   c. How do you act in this situation?

_____

3. Do the Trigger map again, writing the same trigger in the oval. Before you start writing, listen to background sounds and feel your body's pressure on your seat, your feet on the floor, and the pen in your hand. Once you are settled, keep feeling the pen in your hand as you start writing. Watch the ink go onto the paper and listen to background sounds. For the next few minutes, jot any thoughts that come to mind.

TRIGGER MAP WITH BRIDGING

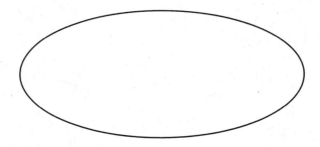

a. What differences do you notice between this map and the previous one?

_____

_____

b. How do you act when exposed to the trigger when your I-System is calm?

_____

_____

_____

Whenever you notice signs of an overactive I-System (such as body tension or memories of your trauma), it means you have more requirements to defuse, many of which you found on the previous map. As you already know, once you have defused your requirements about a trigger, you can face that trigger without an I-System meltdown.

DAY TWO   DATE: _____

1. Whenever a current event triggers your I-System, tune in to your senses and find the hidden require-
    ment. You have defused the requirement when your mind-body bridging practice has helped you
    face past triggers related to your trauma without causing mind-body distress. Now you'll function
    naturally. Log your experiences:

Current Trigger	Requirement	Past Reaction	Present Reaction
Helicopter sound	Helicopters should not fly around my house.	Tight chest, clenched fist, rapid heartbeat, urge to run for cover	Mild startle, mild tightness in chest, keep walking to work

Which requirements were you able to defuse, and how did you do it?

Defused Requirements	Mind-Body Bridging Tools
Helicopters should not fly around my house.	Felt my fingers rub together, recognized my requirement

Chapter 8—Day Two cont.

2. Do a Trigger map. From the previous chart, choose a requirement you couldn't defuse. Write the trigger at the top of the map, and write the requirement that it triggers in the oval. Next, scatter your thoughts around the oval. Write for three to five minutes without editing your thoughts. Describe your body tension at the bottom of the map.

TRIGGER REQUIREMENT MAP

My trigger is

_____

_____

Body Tension:

_____

_____

a. Bubble your map by drawing a circle (bubble) around the thought that brings the most body tension. Take a few minutes to scatter more thoughts around the circled item. Bubble any other troubling items.

b. List your requirements:

_____

_____

_____

c. How do you act in this situation?

_____

Chapter 8—Day Two cont.

3. Do the Trigger map again, writing the same trigger at the top of the map and the same requirement in the oval. Before you start writing, listen to background sounds and feel your body's pressure on your seat, your feet on the floor, and the pen in your hand. Once you are settled, keep feeling the pen in your hand as you start writing. Watch the ink go onto the paper and listen to background sounds. For the next few minutes, jot any thoughts that come to mind.

TRIGGER REQUIREMENT MAP WITH BRIDGING

My trigger is

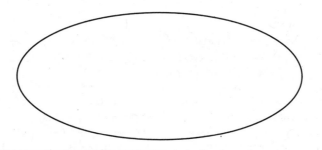

a. Compare this map with the previous one. What do you notice?

b. On this map, the trigger is the same, but your mind-body state has changed. How will you handle the trigger when it comes up again?

It's now clear that your unmet requirement, rather than the event, is what causes your distress. Your ability to find and defuse your requirements is vital for you to heal from your PTSD.

DAY THREE   DATE: _____

1. Keep tuning in to your senses and finding your hidden requirements whenever a current event triggers your I-System. How did it go?

_____

_____

2. Log any troubling behaviors or symptoms that come up during your day related to your trauma experiences; for example, avoiding people or situations; going numb; abusing alcohol or drugs; being easily angered; feeling restless or depressed; being unable to concentrate; or having relationship issues, or work or school problems. What are the current triggering events? Also note your requirement and the traumatic event.

Troubling Behavior or Symptom	Current Trigger	Requirement	Traumatic Event
Yelled at my wife, almost pushed her	Wife asked why I'm not the same as I was before Iraq	My wife should not ask me those questions.	Iraq
Felt numb all over	Saw a romantic movie on TV	I shouldn't see romantic scenes.	Rape
Drank too much	Bad memories	I shouldn't have bad memories.	Child abuse

Chapter 8—Day Three cont.

3. Do a map for a requirement from the previous chart that you've had trouble defusing. Write the triggering event at the top of the map and the requirement in the oval. Around the oval, scatter any thoughts that come up when you think about that requirement going unmet. Write for three to five minutes without editing your thoughts. Describe your body tension at the bottom of the map.

REQUIREMENT MAP

My trigger is

_____

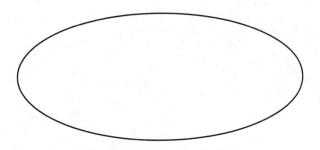

Body Tension:

_____

_____

a. List other requirements you find:

_____

_____

Finding the requirement (*Helicopters shouldn't fly over my house*) hidden beneath the trigger (helicopter sounds) may not quiet your I-System at first, but if you keep it up, bubble mapping will show you hidden requirements like *The medevac helicopter should have arrived before Tom died*. Getting clear about your requirements through mapping helps you defuse the current trigger in real time.

b. Bubble the item that brings the most body tension. Continue to bubble any other troubling requirements.

c. What other requirements did you find?

_____

_____

Chapter 8—Day Three cont.

4. Do this map again, writing the same event at the top of the map and the same requirement in the oval. Before you start writing, listen to background sounds and feel your body's pressure on your seat, your feet on the floor, and the pen in your hand. Once you are settled, keep feeling the pen in your hand as you start writing. Watch the ink go onto the paper and listen to background sounds. For the next few minutes, jot any thoughts that come to mind.

REQUIREMENT MAP WITH BRIDGING

My trigger is

_____

a. How is this map different from the previous one?

_____

_____

b. How do you act in this state?

_____

_____

c. Go back and look at your requirement chart from the start of today's assignments. On a separate sheet of paper, map any requirements you still haven't been able to defuse. Use all the mind-body bridging mapping tools you have learned.

DAY FOUR   DATE: _____

1. Often, our distressing experiences relate to fearful thoughts. Throughout the day, notice what events make you fearful. Find the hidden requirement for each.

Event	Fear	Requirement
Wife was upset with me.	Wife will leave me.	Wife shouldn't be upset. Wife shouldn't leave me.
Nightmare	I'll never be well. I'm crazy.	I shouldn't have nightmares. I should be well. I shouldn't be crazy.

2. List your three greatest fears about your life. Find and list the hidden requirements for each:

   a. _____

   _____

   b. _____

   _____

   c. _____

   _____

Chapter 8—Day Four cont.

3. Do a Fear map, writing your greatest fear in the oval. Scatter your thoughts around the oval for three to five minutes, without editing them. Write about your body tension at the bottom of the map.

FEAR MAP

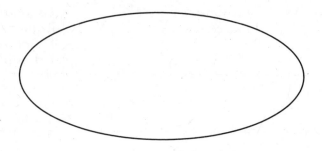

Body Tension:

_____

_____

a. Bubble your map by drawing a circle (bubble) around the thought that brings the most body tension. Take a few minutes to scatter more thoughts around the circled item. Bubble any other troubling items.

b. List your storylines:

_____

_____

c. List your requirements:

_____

_____

   Fear is an emotion from natural functioning that signals you about possible danger. When the I-System captures your fears, it convinces you that you can't cope, which paralyzes you, making you a victim of your fear. Fighting the fear never works. It is helpful to consider the fear as having two parts: a thought and a body sensation.

Chapter 8—Day Four cont.

4. Do this map again, writing the same fear in the oval. Before you start writing, listen to background sounds and feel your body's pressure on your seat, your feet on the floor, and the pen in your hand. Once you are settled, keep feeling the pen in your hand as you start writing. Watch the ink go onto the paper and listen to background sounds. For the next few minutes, jot any thoughts that come to mind.

FEAR MAP WITH BRIDGING

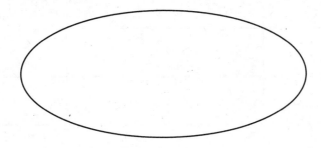

a. What's your mind-body state on this map, compared to the previous one?

_____

_____

b. How would you act differently in this state?

_____

_____

c. Do you think you could defuse your requirements from the previous map next time the situation comes up? Yes _____ No _____

    In mind-body bridging, being fearless doesn't mean you have no fear. Fear is an emotion from natural functioning. To be fearless is to defuse the requirement beneath the fear so that you keep the I-System from capturing the fear and limiting your ability to deal with that situation. When you defuse requirements, rather than react to a fearful situation, you deal with the situation proactively from your naturally functioning true self.

DAY FIVE   DATE: _____

1. List five situations that made you feel fearful, limited, or bogged down by thinking too much. Find the requirement behind each event:

Situation	Fear, Limitation, Thoughts	Requirement
Christmas shopping	Can't go into crowded store.	I should be able to go into a crowded store.
Change jobs	Can't decide.	I should make a decision.
Can't relax, on edge	I'll never be normal again.	I should be normal and relaxed.

The first step to dealing with a situation that makes you fearful is noticing the early signs of an overactive I-System (for example, tension in your shoulders or a knot in your stomach). Next, use your favorite bridging awareness practice (such as listening to background sounds or rubbing your fingers together), and find your requirements.

To defuse a requirement, know that it's your I-System, not the situation (or fear), that's causing your distress. If the requirement you are working with is hard to defuse, understand that there may be other, related requirements you haven't found yet. Doing maps like the following ones helps.

Chapter 8—Day Five cont.

2. Map a situation that left you feeling fearful, limited, or bogged down by thinking too much. Write the situation in the oval (for example, *I need to make a decision about this relationship*). Around the oval, scatter your thoughts for three to five minutes, without editing them. Write about your body tension at the bottom of the map.

FEAR, LIMITATION, OR THINKING TOO MUCH MAP

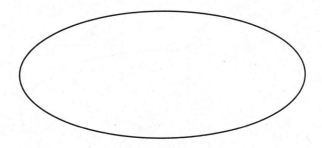

Body Tension:

_____

_____

a. What are your storylines?

_____

_____

b. What are your hidden requirements?

_____

_____

c. Bubble your map if you are still unsettled about anything on it by drawing a circle (bubble) around the thought that brings the most body tension. Take a few minutes to scatter your thoughts around the circled item. Notice your requirements. Bubble any other troubling items.

3. Do the previous map again, writing the same situation in the oval. Before you start writing, listen to background sounds and feel your body's pressure on your seat, your feet on the floor, and the pen in your hand. Once you are settled, keep feeling the pen in your hand as you start writing. Watch the ink go onto the paper and listen to background sounds. For the next few minutes, jot any thoughts that come to mind.

FEAR, LIMITATION, OR THINKING TOO MUCH MAP WITH BRIDGING

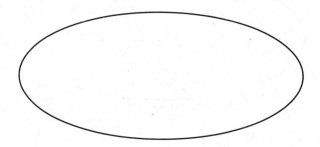

a. What's your mind-body state on this map, compared to the previous map?

_____

_____

b. How would you act differently in this state?

_____

_____

c. How are you better prepared to find and defuse requirements in future situations?

_____

_____

_____

DAY SIX   DATE: _____

1. Tune in to your senses today. Find and defuse your requirements whenever a current event triggers your I-System.

    a. How did it go?

    _____

    _____

    b. List requirements you have defused:

    _____

    _____

    c. List any requirements you still haven't been able to defuse:

    _____

    _____

    d. List any of your daily activities that haven't been freed from the I-System, as well as the hidden requirements for each:

Activity	Requirement
Having a close relationship	I should have a close relationship.
Drinking too much	I should be able to stop drinking. I should be able to drink whenever I want.
Can't stand being with Dennis	I should be able to be around Dennis.

Chapter 8—Day Six cont.

2.   Do a map about one of your daily activities that hasn't yet been freed (for example, *being able to have a close relationship*). In the oval, write the requirement that still needs to be defused (for example, *I should have a close relationship*). Scatter your thoughts around the oval for three to five minutes, without editing them. Write about your body tension at the bottom of the map.

HARD-TO-DEFUSE REQUIREMENT MAP

Daily Activity That Needs Freeing:

_____

Body Tension:

_____

_____

a.   List your storylines that keep the problem going:

_____

_____

b.   List any more hidden requirements you can find:

_____

_____

c.   Bubble map an item that brings a lot of body tension, by drawing a circle around it and scattering more thoughts around it. Do you notice more storylines and requirements? Forcing yourself to do something activates your fixer, but when you defuse your requirements, your natural functioning guides you.

3. Do this map again, writing the same activity at the top of the map and the same requirement in the oval. Before you start writing, listen to background sounds and feel your body's pressure on your seat, your feet on the floor, and the pen in your hand. Once you are settled, keep feeling the pen in your hand as you start writing. Watch the ink go onto the paper and listen to background sounds. For the next few minutes, jot any thoughts that come to mind.

HARD-TO-DEFUSE REQUIREMENT MAP WITH BRIDGING

Daily Activity That Needs Freeing:

_____

_____

a. What's your mind-body state on this map, compared to the previous one?

_____

_____

b. How would you act differently in this state?

_____

_____

c. Write how your natural functioning true self guides you:

_____

_____

_____

DAY SEVEN   DATE: _____

1. Throughout the day, use all your mind-body bridging practices in your life. Notice the triggering events, fears, limitations, excess thinking, and any body tension and mind clutter that comes up with them. Use your bridging awareness practices and thought labeling as you uncover your requirements and storylines. For hard-to-defuse requirements, do a map to find more requirements that hold back your progress. Bubble the map if needed.

    a. How did it go today?

_____
_____
_____
_____
_____
_____
_____
_____
_____
_____
_____
_____
_____
_____
_____
_____

    b. Do you see that you're not a victim of your past trauma? Yes ____ No ____

    When you befriend your I-System, your mind, body, and spirit heal naturally.

Chapter 8—Day Seven cont.

2. Do a Peace of Mind map. Think of what might give you peace of mind. After a few minutes, write your thoughts around the oval (for example, *great job, healthy family, neighbors minding their own business*). Take your time and be specific.

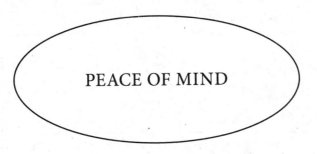

a. With each item, rate the degree of body tension you have when you realize the item *will not* be fulfilled; use this scale: Ø for none, + for mild, ++ for moderate, or +++ for severe.

b. What do you notice?

_____

_____

_____

_____

As you know, the items with plus signs are your requirements. Your I-System pushes the false belief that meeting your requirements gives you peace of mind. You don't need to analyze peace of mind to *find* it. If you do, it's I-System driven. True peace of mind comes after finding and defusing your hidden requirements. Only then can you experience your ever-present wellspring of healing, goodness, beauty, power, and wisdom.

c. Do you understand that the only real peace of mind comes from a calm I-System? Yes _____ No _____

MBB WEEKLY EVALUATION SCALE
DEALING WITH YOUR TRAUMA:
TRIGGERS AND FEARS

Date: _____

During the past week, how did you do with these practices? Check the description that best matches your practice: hardly ever, occasionally, usually, or almost always.

How often do you...	Hardly Ever	Occasionally	Usually	Almost Always
Recognize that body tension, impaired functioning, and trauma memories are signs of an overactive I-System?				
Notice that triggers are upsetting because they fail to meet a requirement?				
Find requirements beneath the triggers?				
Defuse requirements in real time?				
Have fewer flashbacks or strong emotional responses in situations that remind you of your trauma?				
Feel comfortable and less limited?				
Find that you have more interest in the world around you and no longer need to avoid situations as much?				
Realize that by quieting your I-System, you are healing from your trauma?				

List three situations you are handling well that used to upset you because they reminded you of your trauma:

_____

_____

List the requirements you have defused related to the situations above:

_____

_____

List three trauma memories that no longer activate your I-System:

_____

_____

HEAL SECONDARY WOUNDING AND FACE THE FUTURE WITH PEACE OF MIND

An explorer never gets rid of her compass, because its information keeps her on track. Your I-System is your lifelong compass that lets you know when you are off course by giving you the warning signals of body tension and mind clutter. It's critical that you be able to use this information to heal yourself and live your life at its best.

The I-System is a very active system. It's important to know that if you quiet your I-System using your bridging awareness practices *before* you have clearly identified the requirement, the requirement will activate your I-System again in the future, limiting your ability to heal yourself.

This chapter will introduce an advanced, rapid-fire mapping practice to uncover your hidden requirements that we call *power mapping*. This free-association tool quickly expands your awareness of your requirements about a problem, situation, event, or person. Without using your bridging awareness practices, you do map after map, just watching your overactive I-System in action. When you power map, your I-System has free rein, but your true self is still in the driver's seat.

In this chapter, you map your *secondary wounding* experiences. Secondary wounding is when a person says or does something to you that hurts because it relates to your trauma experience. You'll learn that you don't need to fear the future, that it's not your enemy. You'll keep using your mind-body bridging tools to uncover your overactive I-System's myths, limitations, and false self-beliefs. Your ability to quiet and befriend your I-System is essential to your progress. Let's get started so you can have peace of mind and a sense of well-being about your future.

DAY ONE   DATE: _____

1. During the day, notice when someone says or does something to you that's hurtful because it relates to your traumatic event. Complete this chart:

Situation	Body Tension	Requirement	Your Reaction
Mother asks, "How come you are the only one in this family this bad thing happened to?"	Chest tight, pressure in head	My mother should be more understanding about my having been raped.	Feel like curling up in a little ball. Want to get away from her.

Chapter 9—Day One cont.

2. Map your most recent, painful secondary wounding experience from the previous chart. In the oval, briefly write the experience. Then, around the oval write whatever comes to mind. Take three to five minutes. At this advanced stage in your practice, it helps to let your thoughts and feelings flow freely, whether or not they relate directly to your traumatic experience. Don't edit yourself. When you are done, note your body tension at the bottom of the map.

> ## SECONDARY WOUNDING EXPERIENCE MAP

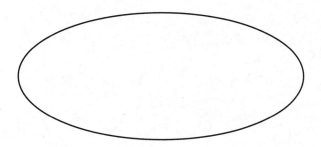

Body Tension:

_____

_____

a. List any requirements you find about the event that triggered your I-System:

_____

_____

_____

b. Bubble your map by drawing a circle (bubble) around the thought that brings the most body tension. Take a few minutes to scatter more thoughts around the circled item. Bubble any other troubling items. As you find more requirements, add them to the list in part a.

c. How do you act in this mind-body state?

_____

_____

3. Do this map again, writing the same secondary wounding experience in the oval. Before you start writing, listen to background sounds and feel your body's pressure on your seat, your feet on the floor, and the pen in your hand. Once you are settled, keep feeling the pen in your hand as you start writing any thoughts that come to mind. Watch the ink go onto the paper and keep listening to background sounds.

SECONDARY WOUNDING EXPERIENCE MAP WITH BRIDGING

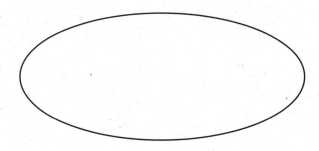

   a. Compare the two maps. What do you notice?

_____

_____

_____

   b. Are your thoughts clearer? Yes _____ No _____

   c. How do you behave in this state?

_____

_____

   d. Are you prepared to defuse the requirements you found on your previous map? Yes _____ No _____

With this map, you saw firsthand that your sense of well-being and peace of mind don't depend on what people say or do, nor do they depend on what you have or haven't been through.

DAY TWO   DATE: _____

During the day, notice when others' behavior upsets you.

1. What body tension or mind clutter did you notice when people didn't behave as you wanted?

_____

_____

_____

_____

2. Uncover the requirements you have for these people:

_____

_____

_____

_____

For someone's behavior that's still troubling you, break down that behavior (for example, *He disrespects me*) into smaller behaviors (for example, *She holds her head up, That look in her eyes, The condescending tone of voice, The way he always has to give his opinion of the Iraq War*). Defusing the requirements that go with the smaller behaviors will help defuse the larger requirement.

3. When you have uncovered your requirements, take a moment to tune in to your senses. What happens to your requirements?

_____

_____

_____

_____

4. Map another recent, painful secondary wounding experience. Briefly write the experience in the oval. Around the oval, write whatever comes to mind. Take three to five minutes. At this advanced stage in your practice, it helps to let your thoughts and feelings flow freely, whether or not they relate directly to your traumatic experience. Don't edit your thoughts. When you are done, note your body tension at the bottom of the map.

SECONDARY WOUNDING EXPERIENCE MAP

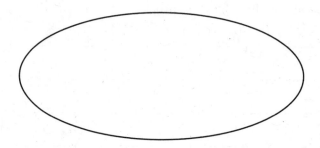

Body Tension:

_____

_____

a. List the requirements you found about the event that triggered your I-System:

_____

_____

_____

b. If you are unsettled about a thought that comes with body tension, bubble map it by drawing a bubble around it. Take a few minutes to scatter more thoughts around the circled item. Bubble any other troubling items. As you uncover more requirements, add them to the list in part a.

c. How do you act in this mind-body state?

_____

_____

Chapter 9—Day Two cont.

5. Do this map again, writing the same secondary wounding experience in the oval. Before you start writing, listen to background sounds and feel your body's pressure on your seat, your feet on the floor, and the pen in your hand. Once you are settled, keep feeling the pen in your hand as you start writing any thoughts that come to mind. Watch the ink go onto the paper and keep listening to background sounds.

SECONDARY WOUNDING EXPERIENCE MAP WITH BRIDGING

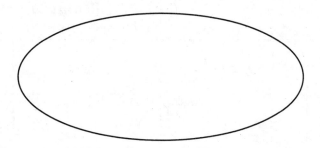

a. Compare the two maps. What do you notice?

_____

_____

_____

b. Are your thoughts clearer? Yes _____ No _____

c. Are you prepared to defuse the additional requirements you uncovered on your previous map? Yes _____ No _____

d. How do you act in this state?

_____

_____

_____

DAY THREE   DATE: _____

Use all your mind-body bridging practices in your life, and notice how your behavior changes. Fill out this chart to see your progress in defusing your requirements:

Current Event	Requirement	Past Reaction	Present Reaction
That guy asked, "How many people did you kill in Iraq?"	People shouldn't ask me about Iraq.	Jaw tense, flushed face I want to punch him.	Frustrated, calm It's too bad he's insensitive.
At work, they call me "sexy."	People shouldn't say I'm sexy.	Shoulders pull up, chest pressure, embarrassed, ashamed of myself	A little tense, don't withdraw, keep working

Chapter 9—Day Three cont.

1. From the previous chart, choose a requirement that you still haven't been able to defuse. Write it in the oval. Next, scatter your thoughts around the oval for three to five minutes, without editing them. Note your body tension at the bottom of the map.

> ## HARD-TO-DEFUSE REQUIREMENT MAP

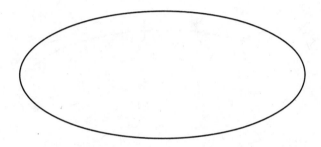

Body Tension:

_____

_____

   a. Looking at your map, list the signs of an overactive I-System:

_____

_____

   b. List your requirements:

_____

_____

   c. Do a bubble map on any troubling thoughts (those that come with a lot of body tension) from the above map to find more requirements. List them:

_____

_____

Chapter 9—Day Three cont.

2. Do the previous map again, writing the same requirement in the oval. Before you start writing, listen to background sounds and feel your body's pressure on your seat, your feet on the floor, and the pen in your hand. Once you are settled, keep feeling the pen in your hand as you start writing any thoughts that come to mind. Watch the ink go onto the paper and keep listening to background sounds.

HARD TO DEFUSE REQUIREMENT MAP WITH BRIDGING

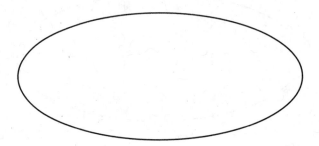

a. How is this map the same as or different from the previous one on the same topic?

_____

_____

b. How would you act differently with a calm I-System?

_____

_____

c. Are you ready to defuse the requirements on the previous map? Yes _____ No _____

d. How will this map affect your life?

_____

_____

Chapter 9—Day Three cont.

3. Power mapping is only for people who have been successful at using mind-body bridging practices in their lives. Use power mapping when your overactive I-System is hard to handle, such as when you have lingering trauma or addiction issues.

    a. To power map, sit down with a pen and pad of paper. In the center of the paper, write the issue that troubles you most (for example, *Depressed, No money, Can't hold it together*). Draw an oval around that issue. Around the oval, quickly write whatever comes to mind. Let your I-System run wild as you jot your thoughts and body tensions. Don't use your bridging awareness practices or try to solve the issue; just watch your overactive I-System in action.

    b. Now take the most troubling thought from that map, write it in an oval on another piece of paper, and map it. Do one map after another by taking the most troubling thought on one map and making it the topic of the next map. Map as long it takes, until your I-System leads you to your hidden requirement.

    When you power map, your true self gains power and strength through your increasing awareness of your damaged self's pressures, urges, and unpleasant body sensations—without carrying out the overactive I-System's demands.

4. Tonight at home, power map the most difficult issue that's still bothering you. How did it go?

_____

_____

_____

_____

_____

_____

_____

_____

This advanced mapping practice shows you firsthand that you can stay in control even when your I-System overheats. If you use in your life what you have learned from power mapping, you don't have to give in to your overactive I-System's demands. You can finally be the one in charge of your future.

DAY FOUR   DATE: _____

The next map can be difficult, but it will show you that you have the strength to face whatever the future throws at you.

1. Do a Sickness, Old Age, and Death map. Scatter your thoughts around the oval for three to five minutes. Please give your I-System free rein, without editing your thoughts. Note your body tension at the bottom of the map.

⬭ SICKNESS, OLD AGE, AND DEATH ⬭

Body Tension:

_____

_____

    a. What is your mind-body state?

_____

_____

    b. What are your depressors, fixers, requirements, and storylines?

_____

_____

_____

    c. How would you live your life in this state?

_____

_____

Chapter 9—Day Four cont.

2. Do this map again. Before you start writing, use your bridging awareness practices. Listen to background sounds and feel your body's pressure on your seat, your feet on the floor, and the pen in your hand. Once you are settled, keep feeling the pen in your hand as you start writing any thoughts that come to mind. Watch the ink go onto the paper and keep listening to background sounds.

SICKNESS, OLD AGE,
AND DEATH WITH BRIDGING

    a.   How is this map different from the previous one?

_____

_____

_____

    b.   How would you live your life in this state?

_____

_____

_____

_____

    c.   Do you see how your overactive I-System's negative storylines about the future keep you from living fully in the present? Yes _____ No _____

Chapter 9—Day Four cont.

3. If a thought on your first map still bothers you (for example, *What will happen to my kids if I die?*), do another map with that as the topic. Write the thought at the top of the map, and jot any thoughts that come to mind. Add your body tension at the bottom of the map.

My troublesome thought is:

_____

SICKNESS, OLD AGE,
AND DEATH

a. From the above map, list the signs of an overactive I-System:

_____

_____

b. What are your requirements and storylines?

_____

_____

_____

_____

c. To find more requirements, bubble map any thought that brings body tension by drawing a circle around it. Take a few minutes to scatter more thoughts around the circled item. Bubble any other troubling items. As you uncover more requirements, add them to the list in part b.

Chapter 9—Day Four cont.

4. Do the previous map again, writing the same thought at the top of the map. Before you start writing, use your bridging awareness practices. Listen to background sounds and feel your body's pressure on your seat, your feet on the floor, and the pen in your hand. Once you are settled, keep feeling the pen in your hand as you start writing any thoughts that come to mind. Watch the ink go onto the paper and keep listening to background sounds.

My troublesome thought is:

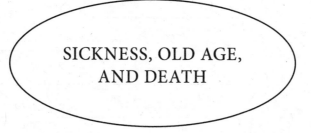

a. How is this map different from the previous one?

b. When your requirements show up in real time, can you now defuse them and live in the present?

Mind-body bridging has been used a lot with cancer patients, working as well on their worst days as their best ones. These patients have learned that when they quiet the I-System, they can always access a wellspring of inner strength and wisdom in their lives.

DAY FIVE   DATE: _____

1. During the day, notice when you feel disappointed with yourself. Note your body tension and your depressors, fixers, and requirements:

    _____

    _____

    _____

    _____

    _____

    _____

    _____

    _____

    _____

2. Do a My Five Most Important Qualities map. Write five of your most important qualities (for example, *Trustworthy*, *Hardworking*, or *Loving*). One or two words will do for each quality. Take a couple of minutes to think about these qualities.

MY FIVE MOST IMPORTANT QUALITIES MAP

    _____

    _____

    _____

    _____

Chapter 9—Day Five cont.

a. Look at your list and cross out the quality that's least important to you. What's your reaction as you imagine yourself without this first quality?

_____

_____

_____

b. Cross out the quality that's the next least important to you. What's your reaction as you imagine yourself without this second quality?

_____

_____

_____

c. Again, cross out the quality that's the next least important to you. What's your reaction as you cross out this third quality?

_____

_____

_____

d. Choose between the last two qualities on your list, and cross out the one that's less important to you. What's your reaction when you cross out this next-to-last quality?

_____

_____

_____

e. Think about the last remaining quality. Cross it out. What's your experience now?

_____

_____

_____

How hard it was for you to cross out these naturally functioning qualities shows how strongly the I-System limits you. It captures your goals and turns them into requirements. It's as if your goodness depends on meeting those requirements. Your reaction when you were crossing out your qualities shows how strongly your I-System tries to define you as a fixed set of qualities. With a calm I-System, your true self is no longer limited to a fixed way of seeing yourself.

DAY SIX   DATE: _____

1. Do a Past, Present, and Future map. In the "Past" section of this map, take two to three minutes to jot whatever comes to mind about your past. Then describe your body tension. Next, in the "Future" section of this map, take another two to three minutes to jot whatever comes to mind about your future. Describe your body tension. Finally, in the "Present" section of this map, take two to three minutes to jot whatever comes to mind about the present and, again, list your body tension.

PAST, PRESENT, AND FUTURE MAP

Past

Present

Future

Chapter 9—Day Six cont.

Let's think about this remarkable map:

a. The "Past" section of your map is full of storylines with themes like *My childhood was bad; I made it through by sheer determination* or *My friends always supported me.* True or not, these stories create spin; they tense your body and take you away from the present. When you recognize storylines in real time, notice that they take you away from doing what you need to do in the present.

　　What do you notice about the "Past" section of your map? List your storylines:

_____

_____

b. The "Future" section of your map has a fixer flavor that's full of requirements. Beside each item that brings body tension, write the requirements you can uncover. For instance, if the item creating body tension is *I won't give in to my urges and cravings,* the requirement is *I should not give in to my urges and cravings.* The I-System has captured your naturally functioning thought, turned it into a requirement, and filled your body with tension and your mind with clutter. When thoughts about the future come up in real time, note your body tension, uncover your requirements, and use bridging awareness and thought labeling to bring you back to the present.

　　List the requirements you notice on the "Future" section of your map:

_____

_____

c. The "Present" section of this map shows what you currently feel and think. Look for signs of an overactive I-System, such as body tension, depressors, fixers, and storylines. Can you uncover your requirements? The I-System has taken stuff from your past and future to try to fix the damaged self. You now know that the fixer can never "fix" the damage, because you aren't broken. You don't need fixing. The damaged self is just your overactive I-System (not what you have been through) limiting your ability to fully live in the present.

　　List any signs of an overactive I-System you find in the "Present" section of your map. Also list your depressors, fixers, storylines, and requirements.

_____

_____

2. Do a Present map. Before you start writing, use your bridging awareness practices. Listen to background sounds and feel your body's pressure on your seat, your feet on the floor, and the pen in your hand. Once you are settled, keep feeling the pen in your hand as you start writing any thoughts that come to mind about the present. Watch the ink go onto the paper and keep listening to background sounds. After two to three minutes, note your body tension.

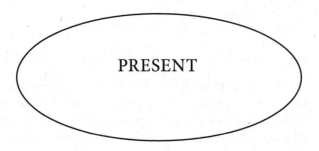

Body Tension:

_____

_____

a. What do you notice about this map that's different from the "Present" section of your Past, Present, and Future Map?

_____

_____

b. Note how you would live your life in this mind-body state:

_____

_____

Being in the present is not being in a zone, nor is it an enlightenment moment or supernormal state of being. Your true self is always present right here, right now. When your I-System is calm, you are in the present. Requirements always take you away from your true self and living in the present moment. If you ever feel *not good enough*, *bored*, *overwhelmed*, *lacking*, or *hopeless*, you have a hidden requirement that's pulling you down and taking over your natural functioning. When your I-System is in high gear, look for your hidden requirement, and use bridging awareness practices to come back to the present moment and what you were doing before.

3. Throughout the day, ask yourself, *Where am I?* which is a simple and powerful mind-body bridging practice. Notice your body tension, mind clutter, storylines, and emotional states, which are signs that you aren't living in the present. Your I-System thrives in darkness, and the light of your awareness is all it takes to shift into natural functioning.

What did you notice today?

_____

_____

_____

_____

_____

_____

_____

_____

_____

_____

_____

_____

_____

_____

You live only in the present. Can your heart pump yesterday's or tomorrow's blood?

DAY SEVEN   DATE: _____

1. Do a The Worst Possible Thing That Can Happen to Me Is... map. Scatter your thoughts around the oval for three to five minutes. List your body tension at the bottom of the map.

```
                    ⬭ THE WORST
              POSSIBLE THING THAT CAN
                 HAPPEN TO ME IS...
                    _____
```

Body Tension:

_____

_____

   a. Looking at your map, list any signs of your overactive I-System:

_____

_____

   b. List the requirements you find:

_____

_____

_____

   c. Do a bubble map for any troubling thoughts (that bring a lot of body tension) to uncover more requirements. As you find more requirements, add them to the previous list.

Chapter 9—Day Seven cont.

2. Do this map again, writing the same thing in the oval. Before you start writing, use your bridging awareness practices. Listen to background sounds and feel your body's pressure on your seat, your feet on the floor, and the pen in your hand. Once you are settled, keep feeling the pen in your hand as you start writing. Watch the ink go onto the paper and listen to background sounds. For the next few minutes, jot any thoughts that come to mind.

THE WORST
POSSIBLE THING THAT CAN
HAPPEN TO ME IS...
_____

a. What do you notice that's different on this map?

_____

_____

b. How do you act with a calm I-System?

_____

_____

c. How will you defuse the requirements on your previous map when they come up during your day?

_____

_____

d. Does this situation disconnect you from your true self? Yes _____ No _____

e. Is it clear that your true self, not your damaged self, can come back whole each moment, no matter what? Yes _____ No _____

MBB WEEKLY EVALUATION SCALE
HEAL SECONDARY WOUNDING AND FACE
THE FUTURE WITH PEACE OF MIND

Date: _____

During the past week, how did you do with these practices? Check the description that best matches your practice: hardly ever, occasionally, usually, or almost always.

How often do you...	Hardly Ever	Occasionally	Usually	Almost Always
Recognize secondary wounding events and their hidden requirements?				
Realize that you don't have to be a victim of what people say or do?				
Have more ease and success in dealing with challenges in your life?				
Realize that only your I-System keeps you from experiencing your wellspring of healing, goodness, power, and wisdom?				
Face the future with peace of mind and a sense of well-being?				

List three secondary wounding requirements you have defused:

_____

_____

_____

List three specific situations where mind-body bridging has changed your life:

_____

_____

_____

MBB QUALITY OF LIFE SCALE

Date: _____

Fill out this MBB Quality of Life Scale and compare it with the ones you did in chapters 1 and 4. The improvement in your scores shows your progress in self-discovery and self-healing. Your dedication and hard work is the key to your realizing that you have always had the power and wisdom to heal yourself. Using your new tools to quiet and befriend your I-System frees you to live life at its best.

Over the past seven days, how did you do in these areas?

Circle the number under your answer.	Not at all	Several days	More than half the days	Nearly every day
1. I've been interested in doing things.	0	1	3	5
2. I've felt optimistic, excited, and hopeful.	0	1	3	5
3. I've slept well and woken up feeling rested.	0	1	3	5
4. I've had lots of energy.	0	1	3	5
5. I've been able to focus on tasks and use self-discipline.	0	1	3	5
6. I've stayed healthy, eaten well, exercised, and had fun.	0	1	3	5
7. I've felt good about my relationships with my family and friends.	0	1	3	5
8. I'm satisfied with my accomplishments at home, work, or school.	0	1	3	5
9. I'm comfortable with my financial situation.	0	1	3	5
10. I feel good about the spiritual base of my life.	0	1	3	5
11. I'm satisfied with the direction of my life.	0	1	3	5
12. I'm fulfilled, with a sense of well-being and peace of mind.	0	1	3	5

Column Totals: ____ ____ ____ ____

Total Score _____

CHAPTER 10

LIFE AT ITS BEST

Congratulations on your dedication and hard work! You are healing yourself of PTSD. Your assignment for this week is to use everything you have learned in this workbook, and do one or more maps each day.

This chapter offers a summary of mind-body bridging practice guidelines and tools, a mapping guide, and a weekly assessment scale that shows you how you are doing. Make copies of the blank scale so you can keep using it after you have finished the workbook. Also, get a blank notebook to use for your maps and for keeping track of the scores of your weekly scales. Although it's best to use your own notebook for maps, in the heat of the moment you can map on napkins, paper bags, and spare pieces of paper. Making a habit of doing maps in your notebook is important for your ongoing progress.

Your I-System is a lifelong companion; manage it well, and you will live your life at its best!

MIND-BODY BRIDGING PRACTICE GUIDELINES

1. Recognize early signs of an overactive I-System:

   ◆ body tension

   ◆ mind clutter

2. Use your bridging awareness practices and thought labeling to:

   ◆ calm your mind

   ◆ release your body tension

   ◆ enjoy your senses

   ◆ create wellness

3. Be aware of your storylines to prevent you from getting stuck in the content of your thoughts.

4. Be aware of your depressor-fixer cycle and your self-belief that you are incomplete and damaged.

5. Map your thoughts, using these tools:

   ◆ mind-body bridging two-part maps

   ◆ bubble maps

   ◆ power maps

6. Find and defuse your requirements.

7. Befriend your I-System and live life at its best.

MIND-BODY BRIDGING TOOLS

Sometimes mind-body bridging is easy, and sometimes it takes a lot of effort. Different tools work for different situations. Using your bridging awareness practices and thought labeling might be all it takes to quiet your I-System, defuse your requirements, and function naturally. Sometimes being aware of your storylines and uncovering your depressor and fixer are what it takes. For tougher situations, use mapping to uncover your hidden requirements. You might need to use bubble and power mapping for those hard-to-find requirements. Whatever it takes, mind-body bridging includes the tools that help you successfully return to your naturally functioning true self.

1. *Bridging awareness practices*—Use them all the time, especially when you notice negative self-talk and body tension. Tune in to your senses by listening to background sounds, feeling whatever you are touching, and looking at what's around you. Simply bring your awareness back to what you were doing.

2. *Thought labeling*—When you have negative thoughts, label them as "just thoughts" and go back to what you were doing. For example, when *I'll never be the same* pops into your mind, say to yourself, *I'm having the thought "I'll never be the same." A thought is just a thought.*

3. *Recognizing the depressor-fixer cycle*—When the depressor traps your negative thoughts that come from natural functioning, it convinces you that you are incomplete or damaged. The depressor and fixer work together to keep the overactive I-System going. When the depressor is in action, enough is never enough, and you are convinced you need to be fixed. Finding your hidden requirements stops the depressor and fixer's cycle.

4. *Storyline awareness*—When you catch yourself mulling over stories, notice the repetitive themes, recognize that there's a storyline at work, and return to the task at hand. It doesn't matter whether or not the stories are true, or whether they're positive or negative. Remember, it's not your negative thoughts that get you down or positive thoughts that pull you up;

it's your storylines, which create mind clutter and fill every cell of your body with tension, supporting the depressor-fixer cycle. When your I-System captures stories, it takes you away from the present, but your awareness is all it takes to bring you back.

5. *Mapping*—Keep a mind-body bridging notebook for your daily mapping. Don't forget, in the heat of the moment, you can map on whatever paper is around.

    a. *Two-part mind-body bridging map*—The first map shows you your I-System in action. Use your body tension to find requirements. On the second map, use your bridging awareness practices to uncover and defuse hidden requirements, putting your true self in the driver's seat. See the mapping guide in the next section.

    b. *Bubble map*—Bubble map to uncover more requirements on any map. Draw a "bubble" around the thought that brings the most body tension. Take a few minutes to scatter your thoughts around the circled item. Keep "bubbling" any other thoughts on your map that come with a lot of body tension.

    c. *Power map*—An advanced mapping practice for people who have a strong mind-body bridging practice, power mapping is for tough problems where you still haven't found your hidden requirements. In this rapid-fire mapping method, you do map after map (without using your bridging awareness practices) to watch your I-System in action. Take a pen and pad of paper, and write your topic in the center of the paper. Draw an oval around the topic, and let your I-System run wild as you jot whatever thoughts or feelings come to mind. Don't try to figure out the issue. Keep doing one map after another by using the most troubling thought on one map as the topic for the next map. Keep mapping for however long it takes, until your I-System leads you to uncover your hidden requirements. Finally the I-System quiets down on its own.

6. *Defusing requirements*—Whenever you experience body tension and cluttered thoughts (like negative self-talk), use mind-body bridging tools to calm the I-System. Next, find the hidden requirement (for example, for the self-talk *I'll never be the same*, the requirement might be *I should be just as I was before*). Then recognize that your overactive I-System is causing your current distress, not current or past events. Making a habit of using thought labeling and bridging awareness tools, along with being aware of your requirements, lessens the I-System's power. Map any hard-to-defuse requirements. You will know you have defused the requirement when you experience a sudden or gradual release of body tension about the situation.

MIND-BODY BRIDGING MAPPING GUIDE

1. Choose a mapping topic and write it in the oval. It may be as simple as "What's on My Mind" or as specific as a certain troubling situation. Next, scatter your thoughts for three to five minutes, without editing them. Describe your body tension at the bottom of the map.

CHOOSE YOUR TOPIC MAP

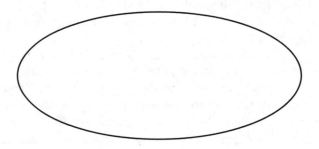

Body Tension:

_____

_____

What's your overactive I-System doing?

    a. What are your depressors?

_____

    b. What are your fixers?

_____

    c. What are your storylines?

_____

    d. What are your requirements?

_____

    e. Make a bubble map of thoughts that bring the most body tension, to find more requirements.

2. Do this map again using bridging awareness practices. Write the same topic in the oval. Before you start writing, listen to background sounds and feel your body's pressure on your seat, your feet on the floor, and the pen in your hand. Once you are settled, keep feeling the pen in your hand as you start writing any thoughts that come to mind. Watch the ink go onto the paper and keep listening to background sounds.

CHOOSE YOUR TOPIC MAP WITH BRIDGING

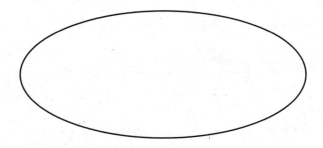

a. How is this map the same as or different from the previous one on the same topic?

_____

_____

b. How do you act in this mind-body state?

_____

_____

c. Are you able to defuse the requirement on the previous map?

_____

_____

Remember, it's either the damaged self or the true self that's in the driver's seat. You choose.

MBB WEEKLY EVALUATION SCALE LIFE AT ITS BEST

Date: _____

During the past week, how did you do with these practices? Check the description that best matches your practice: hardly ever, occasionally, usually, or almost always.

How often do you...	Hardly Ever	Occasionally	Usually	Almost Always
Listen to background sounds?				
Feel the container in your hand when you take a drink?				
Notice gravity?				
Use bridging practices to bust stress or melt misery?				
Become keenly aware of everyday activities, like making the bed, eating, and driving?				
Hear the water going down the drain and feel the water on your body when you are showering or washing your hands?				
Use bridging to help you sleep?				
Use bridging to help you relax and stay focused?				
Notice body tension that points to an overactive I-System?				
Realize that an overactive I-System is causing your problem?				
Recognize your depressor?				
Recognize your fixer?				
Befriend your depressor?				
Befriend your fixer?				
Find the requirements that cause your daily upsets?				
Defuse your requirements?				
Recognize storylines?				
Bridge storylines?				
Recognize the damaged self?				
Experience the damaged self as a myth of the I-System?				
Recognize natural functioning?				
Appreciate your true self that functions naturally moment by moment?				
Appreciate everyday life in a new light?				
Do mind-body maps each day?				

Appendix: Mind-Body Bridging Terms

Identity System (I-System): Everyone has one. When your I-System is turned on (or active), your mind clutter (spinning thoughts) and body tension get in the way of how you live your life and stop you from healing your PTSD. When your I-System is off (or calm), your mind is clear and your body relaxed, letting your body heal.

Requirements: Thoughts or mental rules (or both) about how you and the world should be, requirements are the only things that can turn on your I-System. You recognize them because you get upset when these rules are broken.

Depressor: Helps the I-System stay on. You recognize it by noticing yourself feeling down, and having negative thoughts and a sluggish, tense body.

Fixer: Helps the I-System stay on. You recognize it when you have a sense of urgency and the feeling of being pushed to do things. This pushing is the fixer.

Storyline: Keeps the I-System going. You recognize it by noticing yourself getting caught up in thoughts or stories that pull you away from the world and what you are doing.

Damaged self: How you think, feel, and act because of your overactive I-System.

Bridging (mind-body bridging): Action you take that stops the harm an overactive I-System causes.

Bridging tools (mind-body bridging tools): Tools you use to turn off (or quiet) the I-System so you can heal your PTSD.

1. *Bridging awareness practices:* When you come to your senses by listening to sounds around you, feeling whatever you touch, and sensing your body.

2. *Thought labeling:* When you notice yourself having spinning thoughts, recognize and label them as "just thoughts," and return to what you were doing. This stops the thoughts from making your body feel bad (tense).

3. *Mapping (mind-body mapping):* Doing short exercises where you jot down whatever thoughts pop into your mind about problems, people, and events in your life. Maps help you see the harm the I-System is doing to you so you can turn it off.

4. *Defusing requirements:* Dealing with a situation with a clear mind and calm body, rather than getting upset or melting down when your rules for how you and the world should be are broken.

5. *Befriending the I-System:* When you stop pushing the I-System away and start turning down its volume by just watching it, which makes it into a friend rather than an enemy. In fact, later on, like a friend, it even helps you heal.

Natural functioning: How you think, feel, and act when you are settled.

True self: Who you are when you feel settled about yourself and the world, and your I-System is turned off.

Present moment: Right here, right now—the only place where you can really live your life. It's not a zone, or an enlightened or supernormal state. When your I-System is quiet, your true self is in the present moment.

Wellspring of healing, goodness, power, and wisdom: Source of power that's always with you when you make your I-System your friend.

REFERENCES

American Psychiatric Association (APA). 2000. *Diagnostic and Statistical Manual of Mental Disorders (DSM-IV-TR)*. 4th ed., text rev. Washington, DC: American Psychiatric Association.

Block, S. H., and C. B. Block. 2007. *Come to Your Senses: Demystifying the Mind-Body Connection*. 2nd ed. New York: Atria Books/Beyond Words Publishing.

Block, S. H., S. H. Ho, and Y. Nakamura. 2009. *A brain basis for transforming consciousness with mind-body bridging*. Paper presented at Toward a Science of Consciousness 2009 conference, June 12, at Hong Kong Polytechnical University, Hong Kong, China, Abstract 93.

Boly, M., C. Phillips, E. Balteau, C. Schnakers, C. Degueldre, G. Moonen, A. Luxen, P. Peigneux, M.-E. Faymonville, P. Maquet, and S. Laureys. 2008a. Consciousness and cerebral baseline activity fluctuations. *Human Brain Mapping* 29 (7):868–74.

Boly, M., C. Phillips, L. Tshibanda, A. Vanhaudenhuyse, M. Schabus, T. T. Dang-Vu, G. Moonen, R. Hustinx, P. Maquet, and S. Laureys. 2008b. Intrinsic brain activity in altered states of consciousness: How conscious is the default mode of brain function? *Annals of the New York Academy of Sciences* 1129:119–29.

Menninger, K. 1938. *Man Against Himself*. New York: Harcourt, Brace, Jovanovich.

Nakamura, Y., D. L. Lipschitz, R. Landward, R. Kuhn, and G. West. Forthcoming. Two sessions of sleep-focused mind-body bridging improve self-reported symptoms of sleep and PTSD in veterans: A pilot randomized controlled trial. *Journal of Psychosomatic Research*.

Tollefson, D. R., K. Webb, D. Shumway, S. H. Block, and Y. Nakamura. 2009. A mind-body approach to domestic violence perpetrator treatment: Program overview and preliminary outcomes. *Journal of Aggression, Maltreatment, and Trauma* 18 (1):17–45.

Weissman, D. H., K. C. Roberts, K. M. Visscher, and M. G. Woldorff. 2006. The neural bases of momentary lapses in attention. *Nature Neuroscience* 9 (7):971–78.

Stanley H. Block, MD, is adjunct professor of law and psychiatry at Seattle University School of Law, adjunct professor of psychiatry at the University of Utah School of Medicine, and a board-certified psychiatrist and psychoanalyst. He lectures and consults with treatment centers worldwide and is coauthor of the award-winning book *Come to Your Senses*. He and his wife, Carolyn Bryant Block, live in Copalis Beach, WA.

Carolyn Bryant Block is coauthor of *Bridging the I-System* and the award-winning book *Come to Your Senses*. She is also the co-developer of Identity System (I-System) theory and techniques.

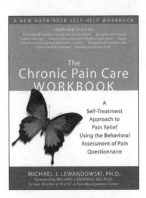

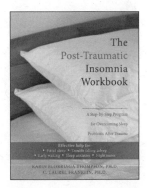